Maths —
No Problem!

English National Curriculum

Consultant Editors
Dr Wong Khoon Yoong
Dr Julie Alderton

Series Editors
Adam Gifford
Andy Psarianos

Authors
Adam Gifford
Michelle Hayfron

D1493008

MATHS
NO PROBLEM!

Published by Maths — No Problem!
Copyright © 2022 by Maths — No Problem!

Printed in the United Kingdom
First Printing, 2022

ISBN 978-1-913458-49-2

Maths — No Problem!
hello@mathsnoproblem.com
www.mathsnoproblem.com

Acknowledgements
The publisher would like to thank Dr Anne Hermanson and Alex Laurie for their contributions.

Preface

Welcome to Maths — No Problem!

Maths — No Problem! is a comprehensive series of textbooks and workbooks supported by detailed online teacher guidance to deliver maths mastery in primary schools. The materials use a spiral design with carefully built-up mathematical concepts and processes adapted from the maths mastery approaches used in Singapore. An integral part of the learning process is the Concrete, Pictorial, Abstract (CPA) approach, which forms the backbone of the materials developed for this series.

Maths — No Problem! incorporates the use of concrete aids and manipulatives, problem solving, group work, individual practice and journaling.

The Maths — No Problem! approach is exemplified throughout the chapters by the following elements:

Worksheet

Worksheets are exercises developed in accordance with the lesson objectives of each chapter which are structured as follows:
Question 1: Knows the basics and concepts.
Question 2: Knows the basics and concepts, and can solve problems in familiar situations.
Question 3: Knows the basics and concepts, and can solve problems in familiar and unfamiliar situations.

Mind Challenge

Mind Challenges are higher-order thinking tasks as enrichment for pupils to apply relevant heuristics and extend the concepts and skills learnt to familiar and unfamiliar situations.

Review

Review follows after each chapter for consolidation of concepts learnt in the chapter. Questions are structured in the same way as the worksheet.

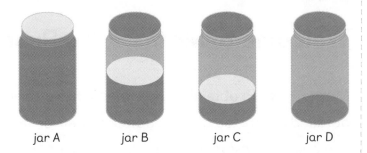

jar A   jar B   jar C   jar D

Revision

Revision provides an assessment of the consolidation of concepts and skills across strands and topics covered in the relevant batch of chapters. Questions are structured in the same way as the worksheet.

Mid-Year Revision

Mid-Year Revision provides an assessment of the consolidation of concepts and skills across strands and topics covered in Textbook A. Questions are structured in the same way as the worksheet.

End-of-Year Revision

End-of-Year Revision provides an assessment of the consolidation of concepts and skills across strands and topics covered in Textbooks A and B. Questions are structured in the same way as the worksheet.

Contents

Chapter 10	Numbers to 40	Page
1	Counting to 40	1
2	Writing Numbers to 40	3
3	Counting in Tens and Ones	5
4	Comparing Numbers	7
5	Finding More or Less	9
6	Making Number Patterns	10
	Mind Challenge	11
	Review 10	12

Chapter 11	Addition and Subtraction Word Problems	
1	Solving Word Problems	15
2	Solving Word Problems	19
3	Solving Word Problems	21
4	Solving Word Problems	23
5	Solving Word Problems	25
6	Solving Word Problems	27
	Mind Challenge	29
	Review 11	30

Chapter 12	Multiplication	Page
1	Making Equal Groups	33
2	Adding Equal Groups	35
3	Making Equal Rows	39
4	Making Doubles	41
5	Solving Word Problems	43
	Mind Challenge	45
	Review 12	46

Chapter 13	Division	
1	Grouping Equally	51
2	Sharing Equally	55
	Mind Challenge	59
	Review 13	60

Chapter 14	Fractions	
1	Making Halves	65
2	Making Quarters	67
3	Sharing and Grouping	69
	Mind Challenge	71
	Review 14	72

Chapter 15	**Numbers to 100**	**Page**
1	Counting to 100	75
2	Showing Tens and Ones	79
3	Comparing Numbers	81
4	Making Number Patterns	83
	Mind Challenge	85
	Review 15	86
	Revision 3	89

Chapter 16	**Time**	
1	Telling Time to the Hour	95
2	Telling Time to the Half Hour	97
3	Ordering Events	99
4	Estimating Duration of Time	103
5	Comparing Time	105
6	Using a Calendar	107
	Mind Challenge	109
	Review 16	110

Chapter 17	**Money**	
1	Recognising Coins	113
2	Recognising Notes	115
	Mind Challenge	119
	Review 17	120

Chapter 18	Volume and Capacity	Page
1	Comparing Volume	123
2	Finding Capacity	125
3	Describing Volume Using Half and a Quarter	127
	Mind Challenge	129
	Review 18	130

Chapter 19	Mass	
1	Comparing Mass	133
2	Finding Mass	137
3	Finding and Comparing Mass	139
	Mind Challenge	141
	Review 19	142

Chapter 20	Space	
1	Describing Positions	145
2	Describing Movements	147
3	Making Turns	151
	Mind Challenge	153
	Review 20	154
	Revision 4	157
	End-of-Year Revision	163

Numbers to 40

Chapter 10

Name: _____ Class: _____ Date: _____

Worksheet 1

Counting to 40

1 Count.
Fill in the blanks.

(a)

30 and ☐ make ☐ .

(b)

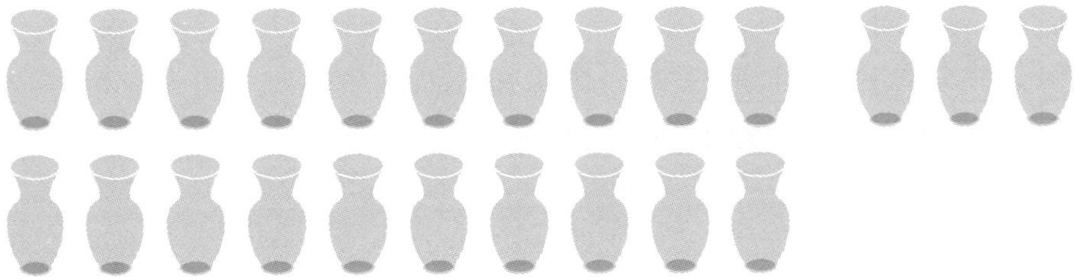

☐ and 3 make ☐ .

(c)

☐ and ☐ make ☐ .

2 Count.
Fill in the blanks.

(a)

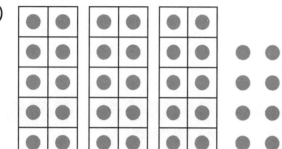

(b)

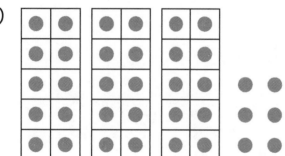

(c)

3 Fill in the missing numbers.

(a)

0   20

(b)

10   20   30

Name: _____ Class: _____ Date: _____

Worksheet 2

Writing Numbers to 40

1 How many are there?
Write in numbers.

(a)

(b)

(c)

2 Say the number.
Write in words.

(a)

(b)

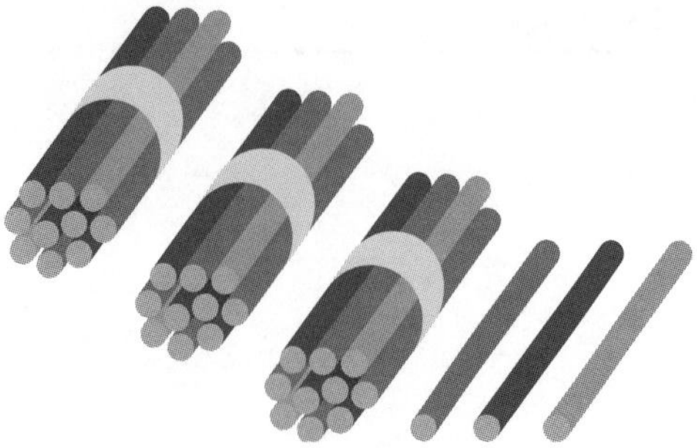

(c)

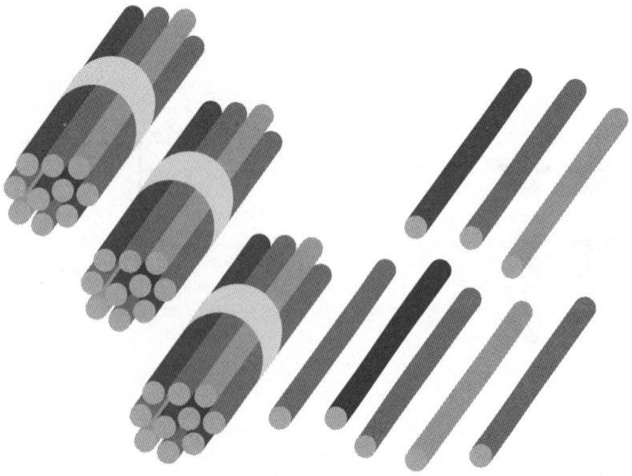

3 How many circles are shaded?
Write in numbers and in words.

(a)

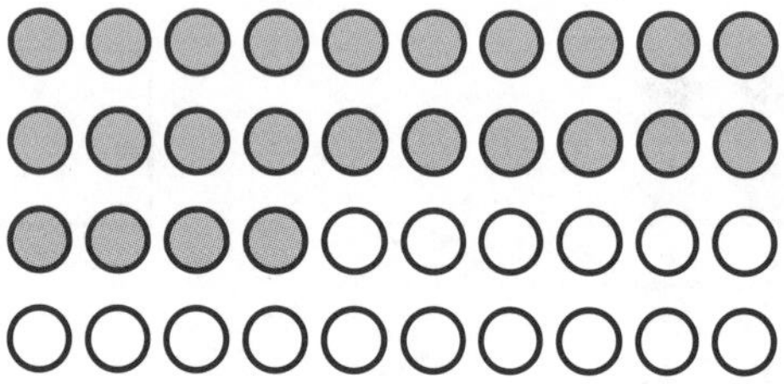

(b)

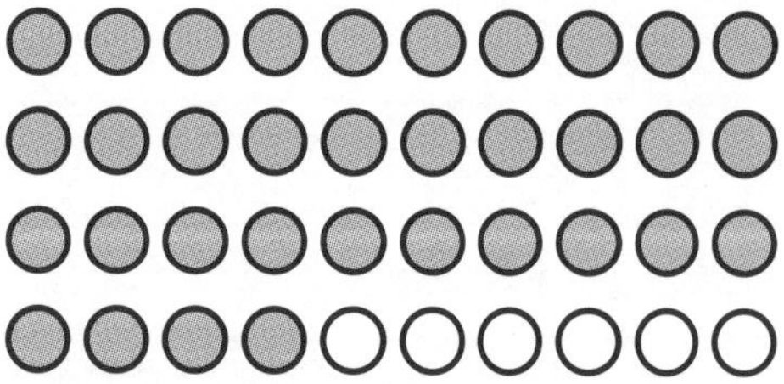

(c)

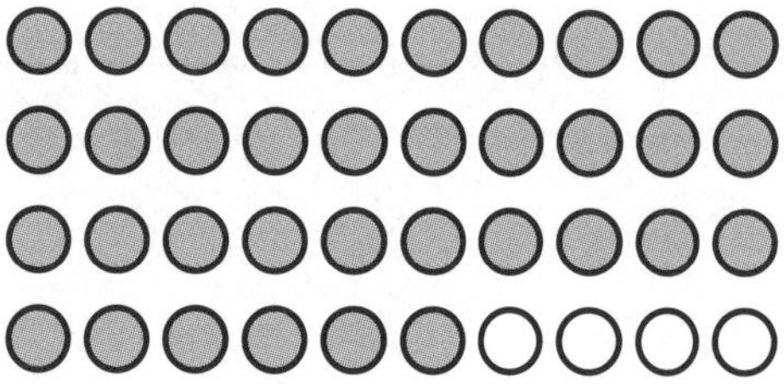

Name: _____ Class: _____ Date: _____

Worksheet 3

Counting in Tens and Ones

1 Count.
Fill in the blanks.

(a)

tens	ones

[ ] tens and [ ] ones make [ ] .

(b)

tens	ones

[ ] tens and [ ] ones make [ ] .

(c)

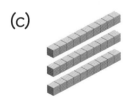

tens	ones

[ ] tens and [ ] ones make [ ] .

(d)

tens	ones

[ ] tens and [ ] ones make [ ] .

2 (a) Write the missing numbers.

(i) 25 = ☐ tens ☐ ones

(ii) 37 = ☐ tens ☐ ones

(iii) 32 = ☐ tens ☐ ones

(b) Write in numbers.

(i) 2 tens 1 one = ☐   (ii) 3 tens 5 ones = ☐

(iii) 4 tens = ☐   (iv) 3 tens 8 ones = ☐

3 Count, then circle the correct number.

(a)

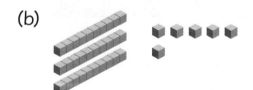

29   39   27

(b)

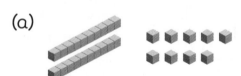

35   26   36

(c)

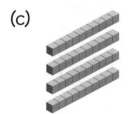

40   30   38

(d)

31   21   32

Name: _____ Class: _____ Date: _____

Worksheet 4

Comparing Numbers

1 Count.
Fill in the blanks to compare.

(a)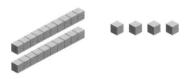

tens	ones

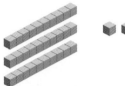

tens	ones

Compare the tens.

☐ tens is more than ☐ tens.

☐ is more than ☐ .

(b)

tens	ones

tens	ones

Compare the tens.
They are the same.

☐ ones is less than than ☐ ones.

☐ is less than ☐ .

2 (a) Circle the greater number. (b) Circle the smaller number.

(i) | 27 | 40 | (i) | 38 | 36 |

(ii) | 39 | 29 | (ii) | 40 | 23 |

(iii) | 28 | 25 | (iii) | 25 | 26 |

3 Compare and order.

(a) Arrange 28, 22 and 39 in order from the smallest to the greatest. Use the number line to help you.

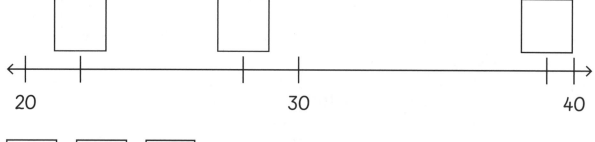

20   30   40

, ,

(b) Arrange 36, 23 and 31 in order from the greatest to the smallest.

The greatest number is .

The smallest number is .

 , ,

Name: _____ Class: _____ Date: _____

Worksheet 5

Finding More or Less

1 Fill in the blanks.
Use the number line to help you.

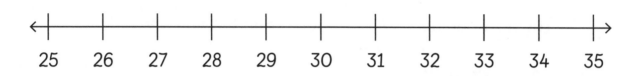

25 26 27 28 29 30 31 32 33 34 35

(a) 1 more than 29 is ☐ .

(b) 1 less than 34 is ☐ .

(c) ☐ is 3 more than 30.

(d) 27 is ☐ more than 25.

2 Fill in the blanks.

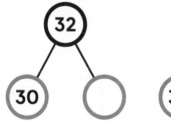 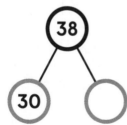

32 is ☐ less than 38.

38 is ☐ more than 32.

3 Fill in the blanks.

(a) 21 is ☐ less than 25.

(b) 30 is ☐ more than 24.

(c) 32 is ☐ less than 39.

(d) 40 is ☐ more than 30.

Name: _____ Class: _____ Date: _____

Worksheet 6

Making Number Patterns

1 Help  describe the number patterns below.

(a) 20, 22, 24, 26, 28

The next number is ☐ more than the number before it.

(b) 39, 38, 37, 36, 35

The next number is ☐ less than the number before it.

2 Fill in the blanks.

(a)
1 less 1 more
☐ 21 ☐

(b)
1 less 1 more
☐ 36 ☐

(c)
2 less 2 more
☐ 25 ☐

(d)
3 less 3 more
☐ 30 ☐

3 Complete the number patterns.

(a) 28, 29, ☐ , ☐ , 32

(b) 23, ☐ , ☐ , 29, 31, ☐

(c) 40, 38, 36, ☐ , ☐

Mind Challenge ▶

When 5 is added to a number it is greater than 35.

When 3 is added to the same number it is less than 35.

What could the number be?

Review 10

1 Count.
Fill in the blanks.

(a)

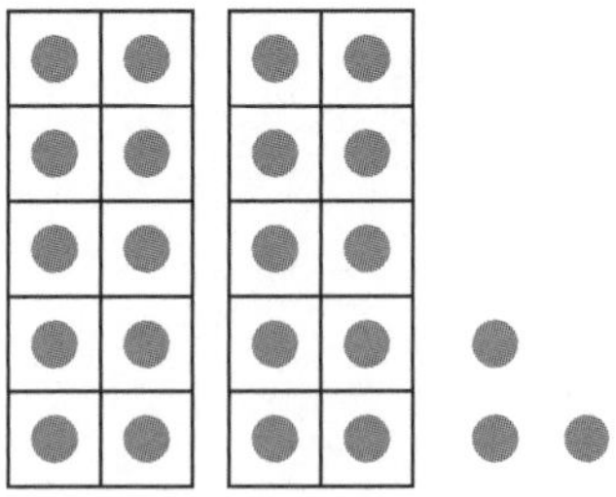

2 tens and ⬚ ones make ⬚ .

(b)

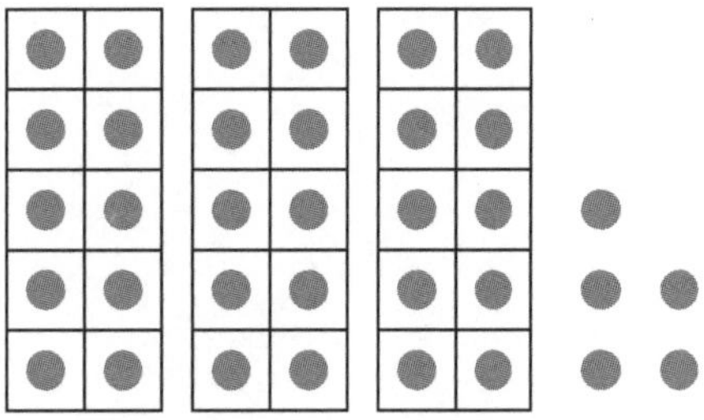

⬚ tens and ⬚ ones make ⬚ .

(c)

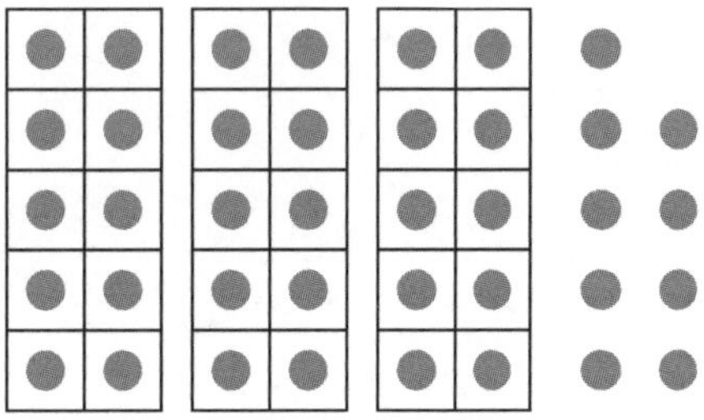

⬚ tens and ⬚ ones make ⬚ .

2 Fill in the blanks.

(a)

tens	ones

(b)

tens	ones

3 Write in words.

26	

4 Fill in the blanks.

(a)

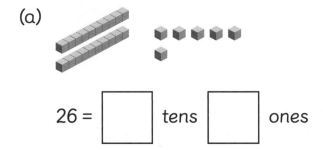

26 = ☐ tens ☐ ones

(b)

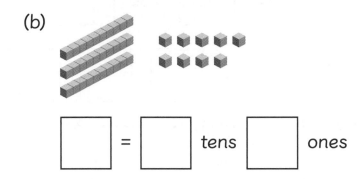

☐ = ☐ tens ☐ ones

5 Find and label the number on the number line.

tens	ones
3	4

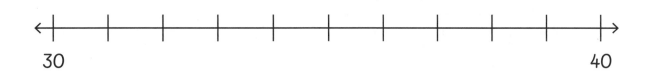

30   40

6 Fill in the blanks with the given numbers.

32   29

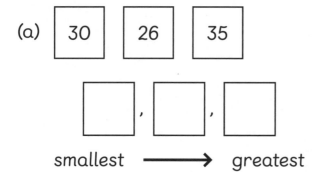

⬜ is more than ⬜ .

⬜ is less than ⬜ .

7 Arrange the numbers in order.

(a) 30 26 35

⬜ , ⬜ , ⬜

smallest ⟶ greatest

(b) 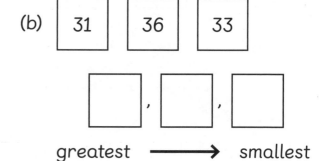 31 36 33

⬜ , ⬜ , ⬜

greatest ⟶ smallest

8 Complete the number patterns.

(a) 29, 30, ⬜ , ⬜ , 33

(b) 27, 29, ⬜ , 33, ⬜

(c) 40, 38, ⬜ , ⬜ , 32

Addition and Subtraction Word Problems

Chapter 11

Name: _____ Class: _____ Date: _____

Worksheet 1

Solving Word Problems

1 (a) There are 7 pencils in the pencil pot.
There are 6 pencils on the table.
How many pencils are
there altogether?

☐ ◯ ☐ = ☐

There are ☐ pencils altogether.

(b) There are 12 balloons.
3 fly away.
How many balloons are left?

☐ ◯ ☐ = ☐

There are ☐ balloons left.

2   (a)   There are 8 boxes of orange juice.
There are 5 boxes of apple juice.
How many boxes of juice are there altogether?

whole

□ ◯ □ = □

There are ☐ boxes of juice altogether.

(b)   Ravi makes 15 sandwiches.
6 sandwiches are made with white bread.
The rest are made with brown bread.
How many sandwiches are made with brown bread?

whole

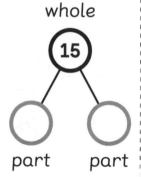

□ ◯ □ = □

There are ☐ sandwiches made with brown bread.

(c) There are no grapes in a lunch box.
Charles puts 9 grapes into the lunch box.
How many grapes are in the lunch box now?

whole

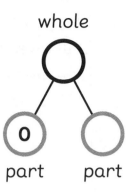

0

part   part

$\Box \bigcirc \Box = \Box$

There are $\Box$ grapes in the lunch box now.

3 (a) There are 4 pots of paint in one cupboard.
There are 7 pots of paint in another cupboard.
How many pots of paint are there altogether?

$\Box \bigcirc \Box = \Box$

There are $\Box$ pots of paint altogether.

(b) Charles has 6 coins in his pocket.
Lulu gives him 6 more coins.
How many coins does Charles have now?

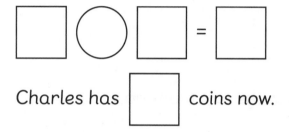

Charles has ☐ coins now.

(c) Sam puts 13 pieces of bread out for the birds.
The birds do not eat any of the pieces of bread.
How many pieces of bread are left?

There are ☐ pieces of bread left.

Name: _____ Class: _____ Date: _____

Solving Word Problems

 1 Use the number line to help you fill in the blanks.

0   1   2   3   4   5   6   7   8   9   10

(a) Lulu's mum needs to make 7 sandwiches.
She has made 5 sandwiches.
How many more sandwiches does she need to make?

5 + ⬜ = 7

She needs to make ⬜ more sandwiches.

(b) Sam's dad needs to make 9 sandwiches.
He has made 3 sandwiches.
How many more sandwiches does he need to make?

9 − 3 = ⬜

 He needs to make ⬜ more sandwiches.

2 Charles needs to put 10 books on the table.
He has put 3 books on the table.
How many more books does he need to put on the table?

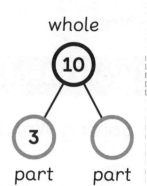

whole

3 + ☐ = 10

10 − 3 = ☐

Charles needs to put ☐ more books on the table.

3 Fill in the blanks.

(a) 10 + 2 = ☐

12 − ☐ = 2

(b) 10 + ☐ = 17

17 − ☐ = 10

(c) ☐ + 5 = 15

☐ − 10 = 5

(d) 14 = ☐ + 10

☐ − 4 = 10

(e) 10 ◯ 3 ◯ 13

(f) 10 ◯ 7 ◯ 3

Name: _____ Class: _____ Date: _____

Worksheet 3

Solving Word Problems

1 Amira's mum sends 17 cards to friends and family.
She sends 8 cards to her friends.
How many cards does she send to her family?

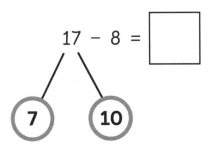

$$17 - 8 = \boxed{}$$

She sends $\boxed{}$ cards to her family.

2 (a) Hannah bakes 15 cookies.
4 are plain, the rest are chocolate chip.
How many cookies are chocolate chip?

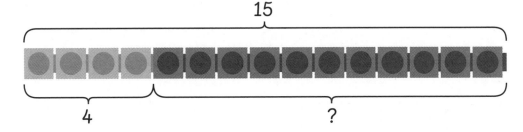

$$\boxed{} \bigcirc \boxed{} = \boxed{}$$

$\boxed{}$ cookies are chocolate chip.

(b) Ruby makes 12 paper aeroplanes.
Charles makes 5 paper aeroplanes.
How many paper aeroplanes do they make altogether?

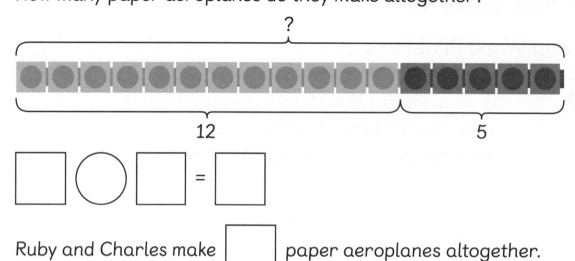

☐ ◯ ☐ = ☐

Ruby and Charles make ☐ paper aeroplanes altogether.

3 After Amira eats 7 grapes, there are 15 grapes left.
How many grapes were there to begin with?

☐ ◯ ☐ = ☐

There were ☐ grapes to begin with.

Name: _____ Class: _____ Date: _____

Worksheet 4

Solving Word Problems

1 (a) Amira and Ravi are playing a game.
Ravi has 8 points. Amira has 6 more points than Ravi.
How many points does Amira have?

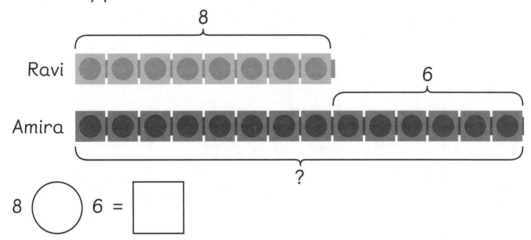

8 ◯ 6 = ☐

Amira has ☐ points.

(b) There are 11 dogs at the park.
There are 5 more dogs than people at the park.
How many people are at the park?

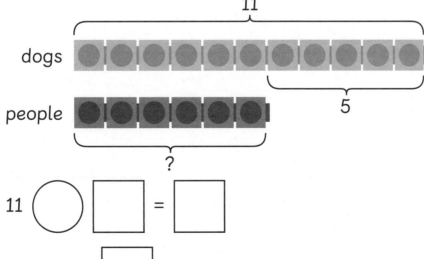

11 ◯ ☐ = ☐

There are ☐ people at the park.

2 There are 12 bananas in a bowl.
There are 4 fewer bananas in the bowl than on a plate.
How many bananas are on the plate?

□ ◯ □ = □

There are □ bananas on the plate.

3 Elliott has 9 cards.
Sam has 15 cards.
Who has more cards? How many more?

□ ◯ □ = □

☐ has □ more cards than ☐ .

Name: _____ Class: _____ Date: _____

Worksheet 5

Solving Word Problems

1 (a) Sam has 14 stickers. Ruby has 9 stickers.
What is the difference between the number of stickers Sam has and the number of stickers Ruby has?

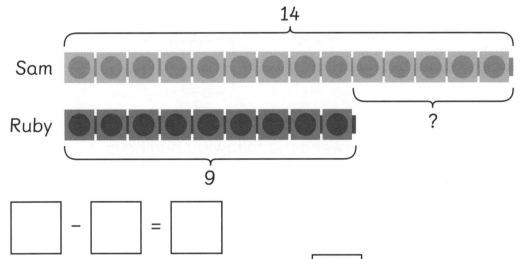

$\boxed{} - \boxed{} = \boxed{}$

The difference between 14 and 9 is $\boxed{}$.

(b) Ravi has 16 crayons. Holly has 7 crayons.
What is the difference between the number of crayons Ravi has and the number of crayons Holly has?

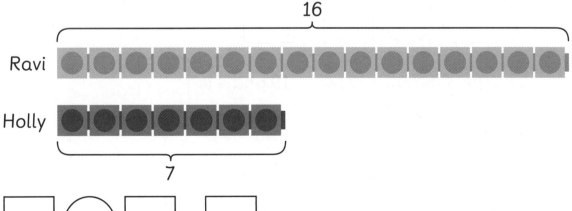

$\boxed{} \bigcirc \boxed{} = \boxed{}$

The difference between 16 and 7 is $\boxed{}$.

2 Oak has 15 keyrings. Jacob has 8 keyrings.
Find the difference between the number of keyrings Oak has and the number of keyrings Jacob has.

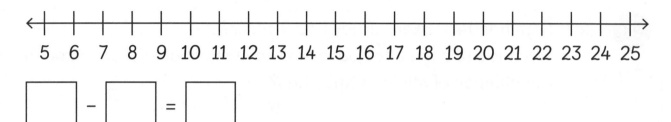

$\boxed{} - \boxed{} = \boxed{}$

The difference between 15 and 8 is $\boxed{}$.

3 Find the difference between the following numbers.

(a) 18 and 5

$\boxed{} \bigcirc \boxed{} = \boxed{}$

The difference between 18 and 5 is $\boxed{}$.

(b) 19 and 4

$\boxed{} \bigcirc \boxed{} = \boxed{}$

The difference between 19 and 4 is $\boxed{}$.

(c) 20 and 12

$\boxed{} \bigcirc \boxed{} = \boxed{}$

The difference between 20 and 12 is $\boxed{}$.

Worksheet 6

Solving Word Problems

Write the missing numbers.

Hannah Sam Holly Charles

(a) (i) There are ☐ between 's 🏠 and 's 🏠.

(ii) There are ☐ between 's 🏠 and 's 🏠.

(iii) ☐ + ☐ = ☐

There are ☐ between 's 🏠 and 's 🏠.

(b) (i) There are ☐ between and .

(ii) ☐ + ☐ = ☐

There are ☐ between and .

2

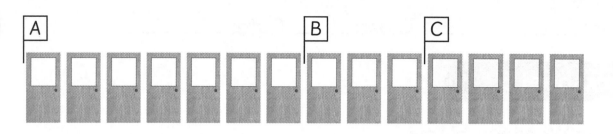

(a) The distance between A and B is ⬜ .

(b) The distance between B and C is ⬜ 🚪 .

(c) ⬜ + ⬜ = ⬜

The distance between A and C is ⬜ 🚪 .

3

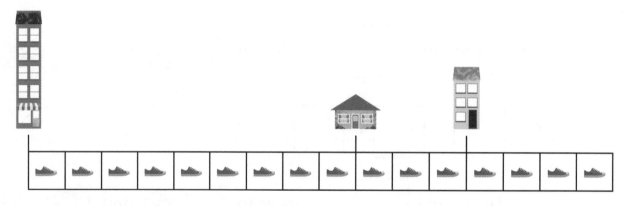

Sam walked from to and then to before he returned to .

What distance did Sam walk?

Sam walked a distance of ⬜ 👟 .

Mind Challenge

There are 27 balls.
9 of them are basketballs, 3 are tennis balls and the rest are footballs.
How many more footballs than basketballs are there?

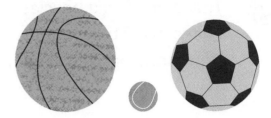

There are ☐ more footballs than basketballs.

Review 11

1 There are 8 red berries.
There are 7 blueberries.
How many berries are there in total?

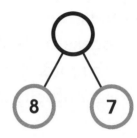

There are ☐ berries in total.

2 Charles has 19 stickers in his sticker book.
Ruby has 4 fewer stickers than Charles.
How many stickers does Ruby have?

sticker book

Ruby has ☐ stickers.

3 Emma has a ribbon that is 13 cm long.
Emma's ribbon is 5 cm longer than Amira's ribbon.
What is the length of Amira's ribbon?

Amira's ribbon is ☐ cm long.

4 Ravi has 16 comic books.
Elliott has 9 comic books.
Who has fewer comic books? How many fewer?

☐☐☐☐ has ☐ fewer comic books than ☐☐☐☐ .

5 Lulu has 7 marbles.
Hannah has 14 marbles.

(a) Who has more marbles? How many more?

☐☐☐☐ has ☐ more marbles than ☐☐☐☐ .

(b) How many marbles do they have altogether?

Lulu and Hannah have ☐ marbles altogether.

6 There are 13 balls in one bag.
There are 4 balls in another bag.
Find the difference between the number of balls in the two bags.

The difference between 13 and 4 is ☐ .

7

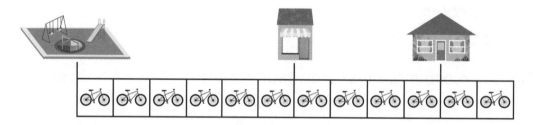

Lulu cycled from the to the  . She then went

from the to the .

What distance did Lulu cycle?

Lulu cycled ☐ .

Multiplication

Name: _____ Class: _____ Date: _____

Worksheet 1

Making Equal Groups

1 Who has made equal groups?
Tick (✓) the correct box.

(a)

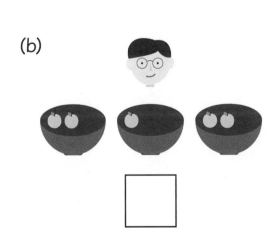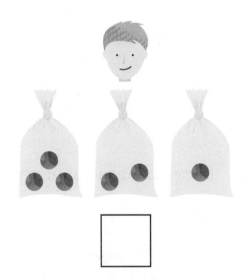

(b)

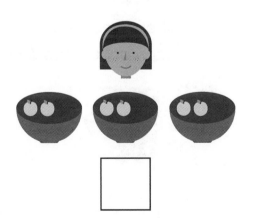

2 Fill in the blanks.

(a)

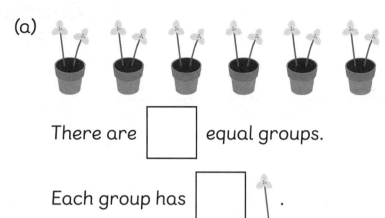

There are ⬜ equal groups.

Each group has ⬜ 🌼 .

(b)

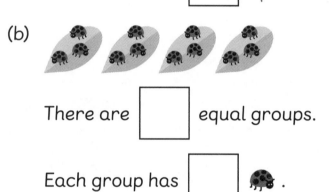

There are ⬜ equal groups.

Each group has ⬜ 🐞 .

3 Draw to make equal groups.

(a)

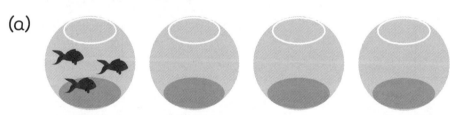

There are 4 equal groups.
Each group has 3 fish.

(b)

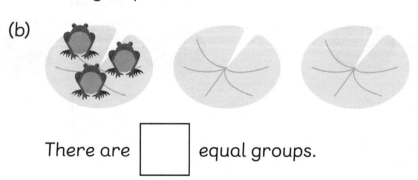

There are ⬜ equal groups.

Each group has ⬜ frogs.

Name: _____ Class: _____ Date: _____

Worksheet 2

Adding Equal Groups

1   Fill in the blanks.

(a)

There are ☐ equal groups.

Each group has ☐ .

☐ threes = ☐

There are ☐ .

(b)

   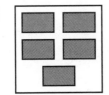 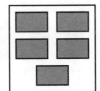 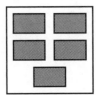

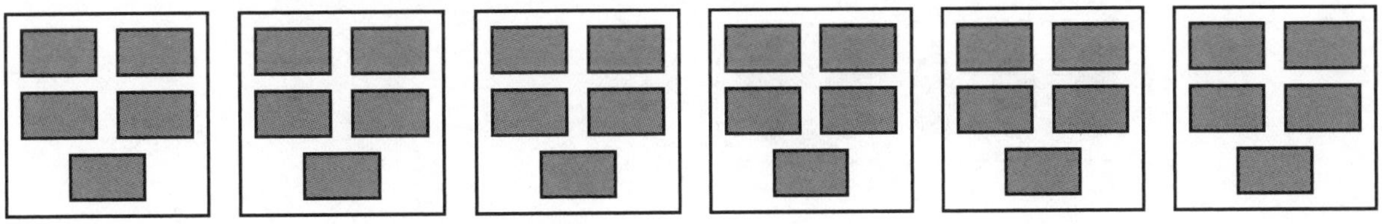

There are ☐ equal groups.

Each group has ☐ ▬ .

☐ fives = ☐

There are ☐ ▬ .

(c)

There are ☐ equal groups.

Each group has ☐ .

☐ eights = ☐

There are ☐ .

2 Make equal groups.
Write the missing numbers.

(a)

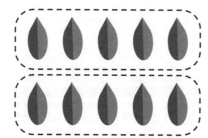

There are ☐ groups of 5.

☐ fives = 10

There are 10 leaves.

(b)

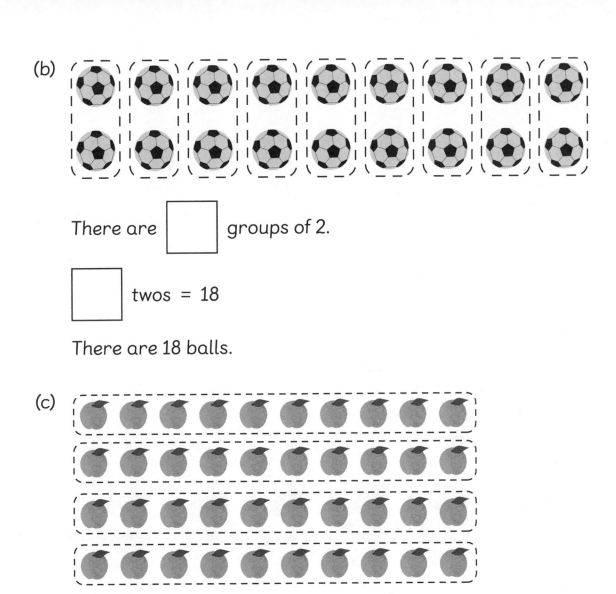

There are ☐ groups of 2.

☐ twos = 18

There are 18 balls.

(c)

There are ☐ groups of 10.

☐ tens = 40

There are 40 peaches.

3 Write the missing numbers.

(a)

⬜ groups of 3 = ⬜

⬜ threes = ⬜

There are ⬜ buttons.

(b)

⬜ groups of 2 = ⬜

⬜ twos = ⬜

There are ⬜ cherries.

Name: _____ Class: _____ Date: _____

Worksheet 3

Making Equal Rows

1 Draw X to make 3 more equal rows.

X X X X X X X

2 Fill in the blanks.

There are ☐  in one row.

There are ☐ rows.

5 ☐ = ☐

There are ☐  in total.

3 Match.

5 rows of 4

•

•

2 rows of 3

•

•

4 rows of 5

•

•

2 rows of 10

•

•

3 rows of 2

•

•
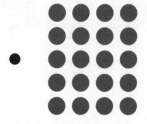

Chapter 12 | Worksheet 3: Making Equal Rows

Worksheet 4

Making Doubles

1 Draw the matching number of spots on each butterfly.

(a)

double 2 = ☐

(b)

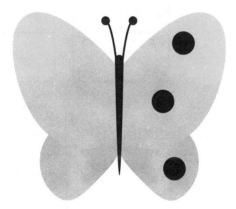

double 3 = ☐

(c)

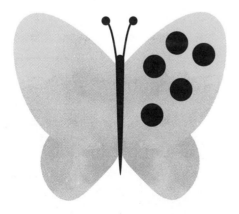

double 5 = ☐

(d)

double 6 = ☐

2 Make doubles and fill in the blanks.

(a)

double 7 = ☐ sevens

= ☐

(b)

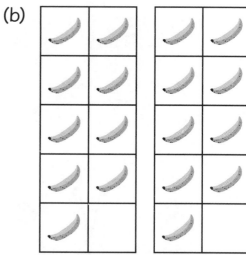

double 9 = ☐ nines

= ☐

3 Find the doubles.

(a) double 8 = ☐

(b) double 4 = ☐

(c) double 9 = ☐

(d) double 10 = ☐

Name: _____ Class: _____ Date: _____

Solving Word Problems

1 (a) There are 3 baskets.
There are 5 eggs in each basket.
How many eggs are there altogether?

[ ] groups of [ ] eggs = [ ] eggs

There are [ ] eggs altogether.

(b) There are 10 tubes of tennis balls.
There are 3 tennis balls in each tube.
How many tennis balls are there in total?

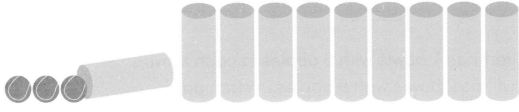

[ ] groups of [ ] tennis balls = [ ] tennis balls

There are [ ] tennis balls in total.

2 (a) There are 4 purses.
Each purse holds 10 coins.
How many coins are there altogether?

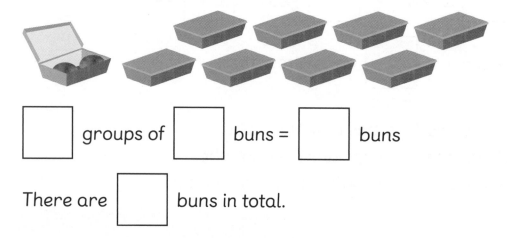

☐ groups of ☐ coins = ☐ coins

There are ☐ coins altogether.

(b) There are 9 boxes.
There are 2 buns in each box.
How many buns are there in total?

☐ groups of ☐ buns = ☐ buns

There are ☐ buns in total.

3 Elliott has 4 bowls with 5 apples in each bowl.
Ravi has 2 bowls with 9 apples in each bowl.

Who has more apples? ☐

Explain your answer using words and pictures.

Name: _____ Class: _____ Date: _____

Sam has 5 equal groups of marbles.
Holly has 3 equal groups of marbles.
Holly has more marbles than Sam.
Both Sam and Holly have less than 40 marbles each.

How many marbles could Holly have in total?

She has ☐ equal groups of ☐ .

Holly could have ☐ marbles in total.

How many marbles could Sam have in total?

He has ☐ equal groups of ☐ .

Sam could have ☐ marbles in total.

Name: _____ Class: _____ Date: _____

Review 12

1 Fill in the blanks.

(a)

There are ☐ plates.

There are ☐ brownies on each plate.

☐ threes = ☐

There are ☐ brownies altogether.

(b)

There are ☐ fields.

There are ☐ sheep in each field.

☐ fives = ☐

There are ☐ sheep in total.

(c)

There are ☐ bundles.

There are ☐ straws in each bundle.

☐ tens = ☐

There are ☐ straws in total.

2 Write the missing numbers.

(a) Ruby has 2 plates.
She wants to have 7 sandwiches on each plate.
How many sandwiches must she make?

Ruby must make ☐ sandwiches.

(b) Amira is arranging her stickers in rows.
She wants to make 3 rows of 6 stickers.
How many stickers does she need?

Amira needs ☐ stickers.

(c) Elliott has 3 buckets.
He wants to fill each bucket with 5 tennis balls.
How many tennis balls does he need?

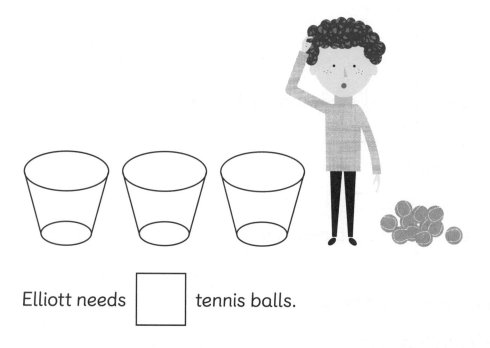

Elliott needs [ ] tennis balls.

3

I can make 5 groups of 4 with 20 marbles.

Charles

I can make 4 groups of 5 with 20 marbles.

Hannah

Who is correct?
Explain your answer.

4   (a)   Draw the matching number of spots on each ladybird.

(i)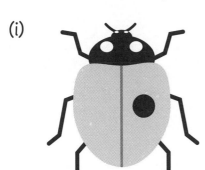

double 1 = ☐

(ii)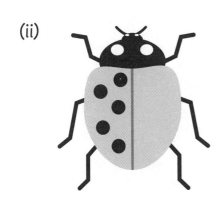

double 5 = ☐

(iii)

double 8 = ☐

(b)   Fill in the blanks.

(i)   double 4 = ☐

(ii)   double 7 = ☐

5 Solve.

(a)

A duck has ☐ feet.

There are ☐ ducks paddling.

How many feet are there in total?

There are ☐ feet in total.

(b)

There are 4 yoghurts in a pack.
There are 5 packs of yoghurt in a box.
How many yoghurts are there in the box?

There are ☐ yoghurts in the box.

Division

Chapter 13

Name: _____ Class: _____ Date: _____

Worksheet 1

Grouping Equally

1 Write the missing numbers.

(a) Jacob has 16 apples.
He puts 4 apples in each bag.
How many bags does Jacob need?

Jacob needs ☐ bags.

(b) Hannah has 24 eggs.
She puts 6 eggs in each carton.
How many cartons does Hannah need?

Hannah needs ☐ cartons.

2 There are 20 counters.

(a) Circle to show groups of 2 counters.

There are ⬜ groups of 2 counters.

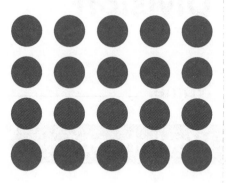

(b) Circle to show groups of 4 counters.

There are ⬜ groups of 4 counters.

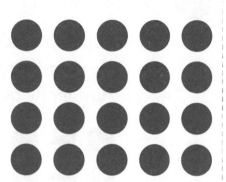

(c) Circle to show groups of 5 counters.

There are ⬜ groups of 5 counters.

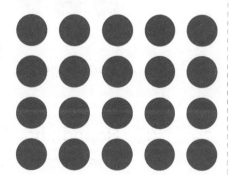

3 Write the missing numbers.

(a) Amira has 16 cherries.
She wants to put 2 cherries on each cupcake.
How many cupcakes should she bake?

Amira should bake [ ] cupcakes.

(b) Ravi has 20 blocks.
He wants to build towers that are 4 blocks high.
How many towers can he build?

I want to use up all the blocks.

Ravi can build [ ] towers.

(c) Charles and Lulu each have 15 counters.

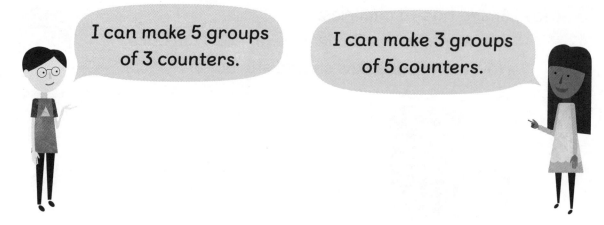

Are both Charles and Lulu correct?
Explain your answer using words and pictures.

Name: _____ Class: _____ Date: _____

Worksheet 2

Sharing Equally

Write the missing numbers.

1 (a) There are 15 sweets.
Put them equally into 5 bowls.

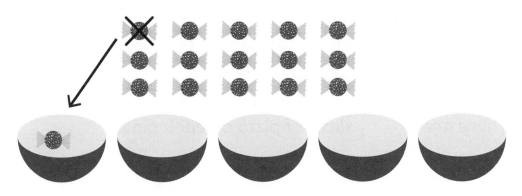

There are ☐ sweets in each bowl.

(b) There are 14 scoops of ice cream.
Put them equally onto 7 cones.

Each cone has ☐ scoops of ice cream.

(c)   There are 12 slices of pizza.
        Put them equally onto 4 plates.

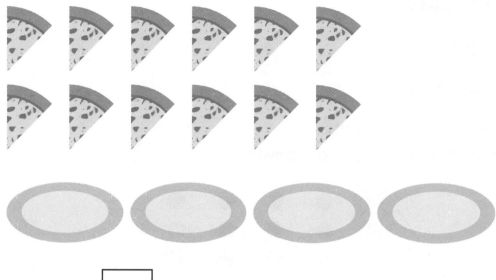

There are ☐ slices of pizza on each plate.

2   (a)   Oak has 9 pencils.
        She puts them equally into 3 pots.
        How many pencils are in each pot?

There are ☐ pencils in each pot.

(b) Ruby has 14 books.
She places them equally onto 2 shelves.
How many books are on each shelf?

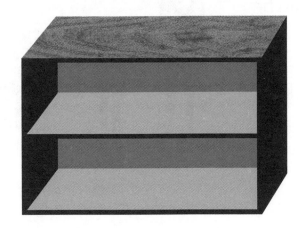

There are ☐ books on each shelf.

③ (a) Mrs Diaz wants to place 24 pens
equally on 6 tables.
How many pens should she put on
each table?

There are ☐ pens.

There are ☐ tables.

Mrs Diaz should put ☐ pens on each table.

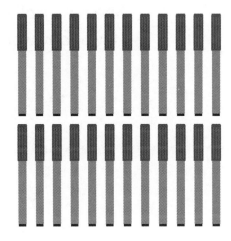

(b) Mrs Diaz has 30 textbooks.
     She asks Elliott to place them
     equally onto 5 shelves.
     How many textbooks should he
     place on each shelf?

There are [   ] textbooks.

There are [   ] shelves.

Elliott should place [   ] textbooks on each shelf.

(c) Mrs Diaz also has 30 workbooks.
     She asks Holly to place them equally onto 2 shelves.
     How many workbooks should she place on each shelf?

Holly should place [   ] workbooks on each shelf.

Name: _____ Class: _____ Date: _____

There are 30 children going to the swimming pool.

The minibus carries 10 children on each trip to the swimming pool.

How many trips does the minibus driver make to get

all the children to the swimming pool?

The minibus driver makes ☐ trips.

Review 13

1 Fill in the blanks.

(a) Circle groups of 4.

There are ☐ groups of 4 toy soldiers.

(b) Circle groups of 7.

There are ☐ groups of 7 toy dinosaurs.

2 Draw the objects in the containers to show equal groups.
Fill in the blanks.

(a) There are 15 fish.
Place them equally into 5 bowls.

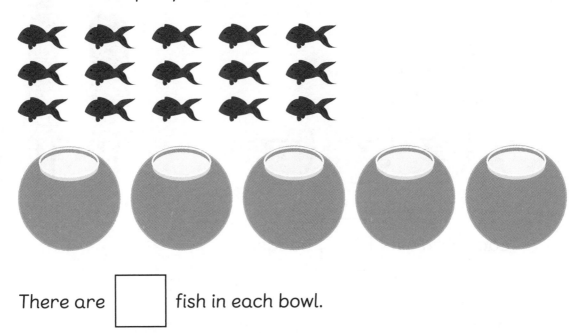

There are ⬚ fish in each bowl.

(b) There are 20 strawberries.
Place them equally into 4 boxes.

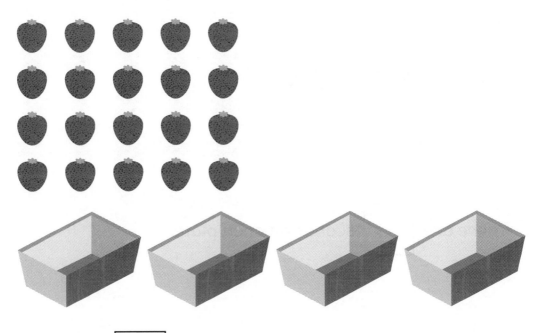

There are ⬚ strawberries in each box.

3 Write the missing numbers.

(a) There are 3 children.
They share 6 badges equally.
How many badges does each child get?

Each child gets ☐ badges.

(b) Holly places 18 scones equally onto 6 plates.
How many scones are on each plate?

There are ☐ scones on each plate.

4 Fill in the blanks.

The muffins can be put in:

☐ groups of 4 muffins.

☐ groups of 6 muffins.

4 groups of ☐ muffins.

6 groups of ☐ muffins.

1 group of ☐ muffins.

5 Match.

3 groups of 2 •

•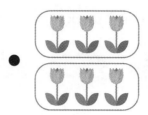

•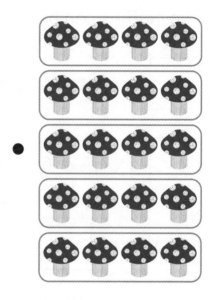

5 groups of 4 •

•

4 groups of 5 •

•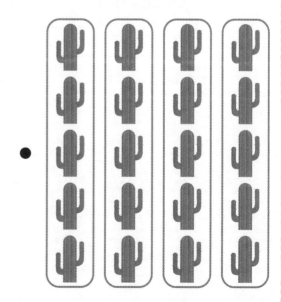

2 groups of 3 •

Fractions

Name: _____ Class: _____ Date: _____

Worksheet 1

Making Halves

1 Circle the shapes that show shaded halves.

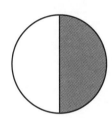 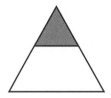 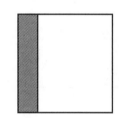

2 Shade to show half of each shape.

(a)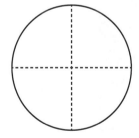

(b)

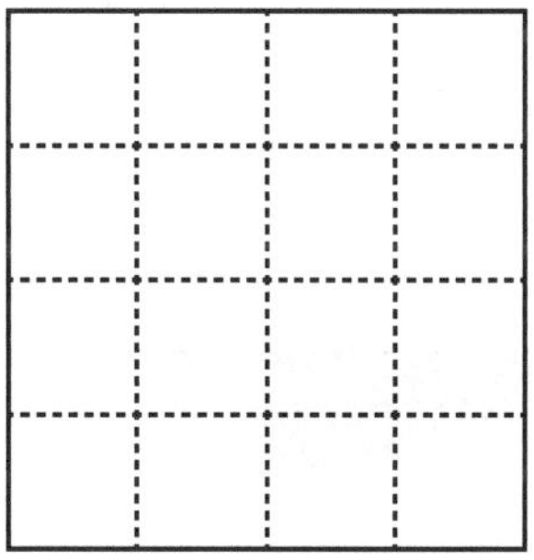

(c)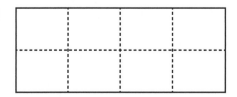

(d)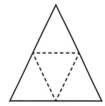

3 Circle the shapes that show shaded halves.

(a)

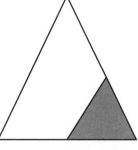

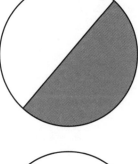

(b)

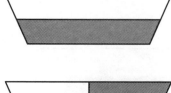

(c)

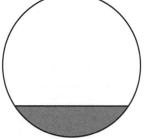

(d)

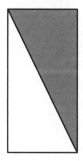

Worksheet 2

Making Quarters

1   Circle the shapes that show shaded quarters.

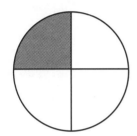
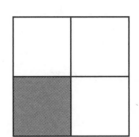
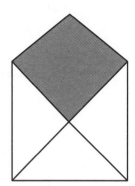

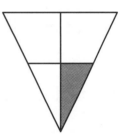

2   Shade to show a quarter of each shape.

(a)
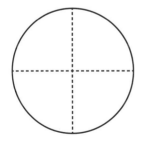

(b)
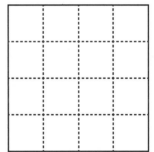

(c)
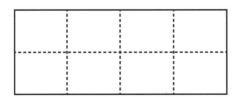

(d)
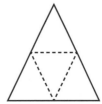

3 Complete the sentences.

(a) ☐ halves make 1 whole.

(b) ☐ quarters make 1 whole.

(c) ☐ quarters make 1 half.

(d) A strip of paper is 8 cm long.

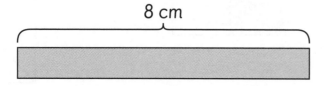

8 cm

When it is cut in half, each piece is ☐ cm long.

When it is cut into quarters, each piece is ☐ cm long.

Name: _____ Class: _____ Date: _____

Worksheet 3

Sharing and Grouping

1 Help write the missing numbers.

(a)

Sam takes half of the bananas.

Sam takes ☐ bananas.

(b)

Lulu gives away half of her comic books.

Lulu now has ☐ comic books.

2 Write the missing numbers.

Amira has a box of cookies.
Half of the cookies are chocolate.
A quarter of the cookies are vanilla.

There are chocolate cookies.

There are vanilla cookies.

3 Write the missing numbers.

(a) These are half the crayons has.

How many crayons does he have in total?

He has ☐ crayons in total.

(b) These are a quarter of the stickers has on a page.

How many stickers does she have on a page altogether?

She has ☐ stickers altogether.

Name: _____ Class: _____ Date: _____

Three oranges are cut into quarters.
How many pieces of orange are there altogether?

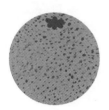 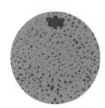 

There are ☐ pieces of orange altogether.

Review 14

1 Shade half of each shape.

(a)

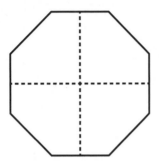

(b)

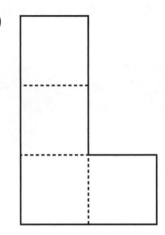

2 Shade a quarter of each shape.

(a)

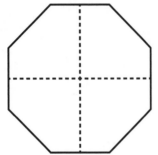

(b)

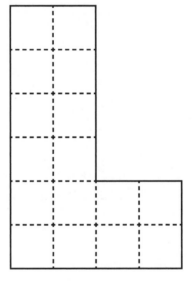

3 Write the missing numbers.

(a) There are 18 fish.
Draw a circle around half of the fish.

Half of 18 fish is ☐ fish.

(b) There are 22 toy cars.
Half of them belong to Emma.
How many toy cars belong to Emma?

☐ toy cars belong to Emma.

4 Write the missing numbers.

(a) A shop has 24 peaches.
Hannah and her dad buy a quarter of the peaches.
How many peaches do they buy?

They buy [ ] peaches.

(b) There are 32 muffins.
A quarter of them are lemon muffins.
How many lemon muffins are there?

There are [ ] lemon muffins.

Numbers to 100

Name: _____ Class: _____ Date: _____

Worksheet 1

Counting to 100

1 (a) Help  circle to make tens and fill in the blanks.

(i)

☐ tens = ☐

(ii)

☐ tens = ☐

(iii)

□ tens = □

(b) Count and fill in the blanks.

(i)
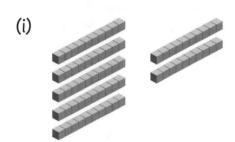

□ tens = □

(ii)

□ tens = □

2 Count then match to a number.

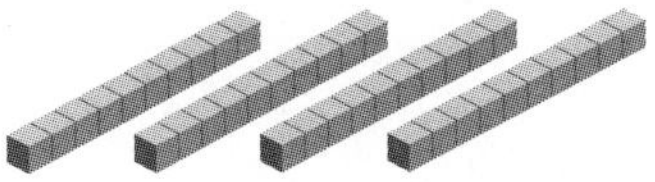

4 rods • • 90

7 rods • • 100

5 rods • • 50

8 rods • • 80

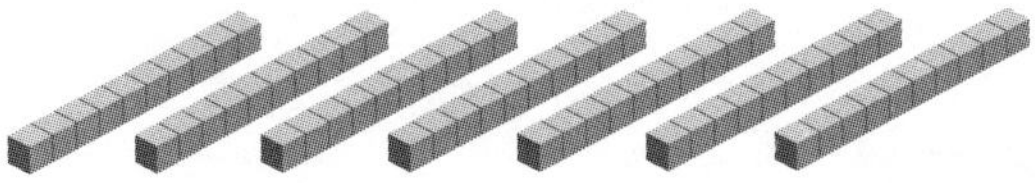

10 rods • • 40

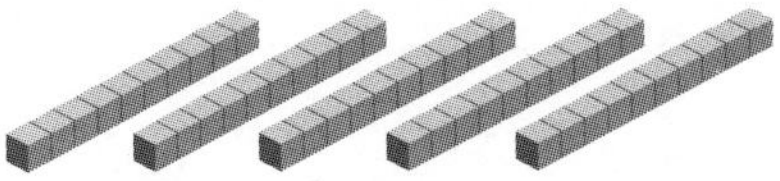

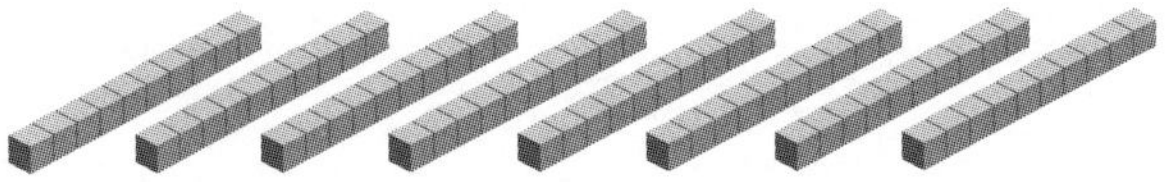

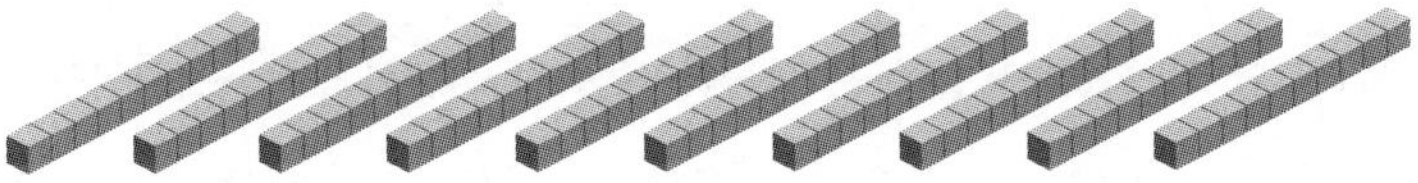

9 rods • • 70

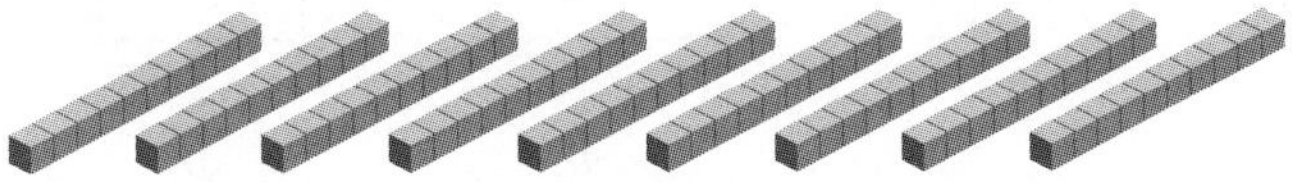

3 (a) Count.
Write in numbers.

(i)

(ii)

(iii)

(iv)

(v)

(b) Fill in the missing numbers.

(i)
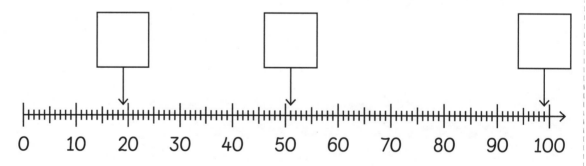

(ii)
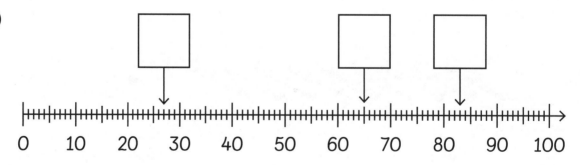

Chapter 15 | Worksheet 1: Counting to 100

Worksheet 2

Showing Tens and Ones

1 Help 👓 count in ten and ones and write the missing numbers.

(a)

tens	ones
2	

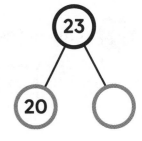

23 = 2 tens and ☐ ones

(b)

tens	ones
	4

☐ = ☐ tens and 4 ones

2 Count in tens and ones and fill in the blanks.

(a)
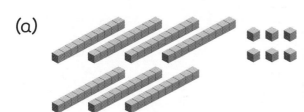

tens	ones

76 = ☐ tens and ☐ ones

(b)

tens	ones

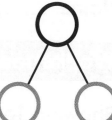

☐ = ☐ tens and ☐ ones

3 Fill in the blanks.

(a) 82

tens	ones

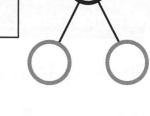

☐ = ☐ tens and ☐ ones

(b) 99

tens	ones

☐ = ☐ tens and ☐ ones

(c) The value of 6 in 61 is ☐.

(d) The value of 8 in 38 is ☐.

Worksheet 3

Comparing Numbers

1   Help  count and fill in the blanks.

(a)

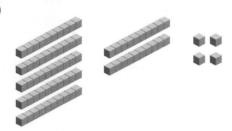

☐ = ☐ tens ☐ ones

☐ = ☐ tens ☐ ones

☐ is more than ☐ .

☐ is less than ☐ .

(b)

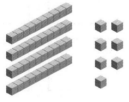

☐ = ☐ tens ☐ ones

☐ = ☐ tens ☐ ones

☐ is more than ☐ .

☐ is less than ☐ .

2 (a) Circle the smallest number.

(i)

| 79 | 97 | 61 |

(ii)

| 68 | 53 | 59 |

(b) Circle the greatest number.

(i)

| 62 | 26 | 57 |

(ii)

| 75 | 89 | 91 |

3 (a) Arrange the numbers in order from smallest to greatest.

(i)   49, 31, 52

⬜ , ⬜ , ⬜

(ii)   66, 75, 65

⬜ , ⬜ , ⬜

(b) Arrange the numbers in order from greatest to smallest.

(i)   23, 32, 22

⬜ , ⬜ , ⬜

(ii)   78, 91, 89

⬜ , ⬜ , ⬜

Name: _____ Class: _____ Date: _____

Making Number Patterns

1 Complete the number patterns.

(a) 72, 73, 74, ⬜ , 76, ⬜

(b) 69, 68, ⬜ , 66, ⬜ , 64

(c) 80, ⬜ , 84, 86, ⬜ , 90

(d) 55, 57, ⬜ , ⬜ , 63, 65

(e) ⬜ , 80, 70, ⬜ , 50, 40

2 Fill in the blanks.

(a)

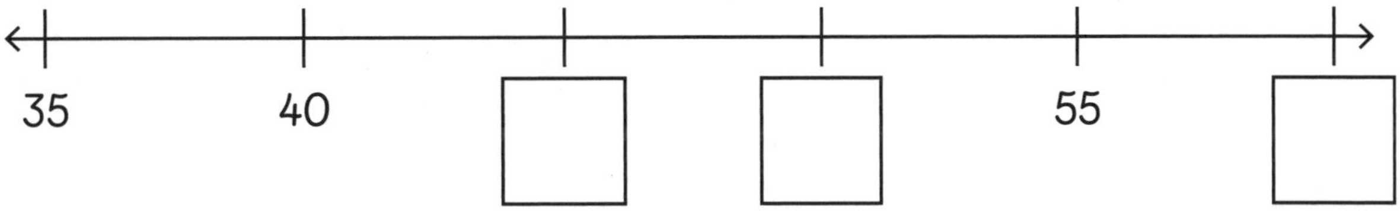

35   40   ⬜   ⬜   55   ⬜

(b)

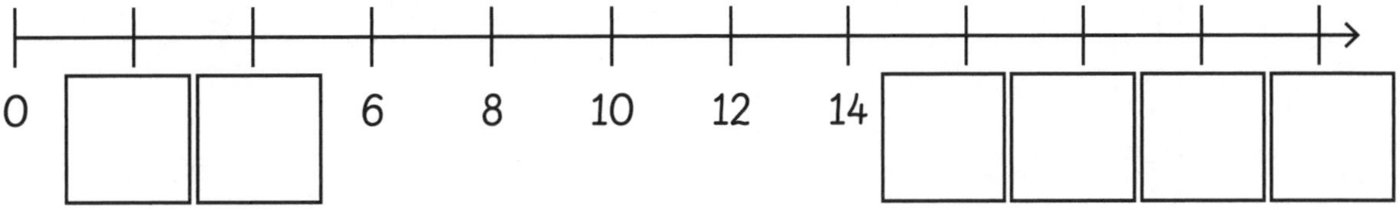

0   ⬜ ⬜   6   8   10   12   14   ⬜ ⬜ ⬜ ⬜

(c)

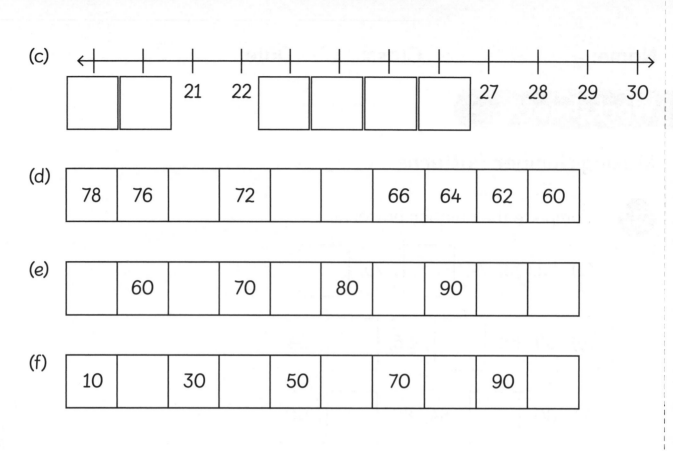

| | | 21 | 22 | | | | | 27 | 28 | 29 | 30 |

(d)

| 78 | 76 | | 72 | | | 66 | 64 | 62 | 60 |

(e)

| | 60 | | 70 | | 80 | | 90 | | |

(f)

| 10 | | 30 | | 50 | | 70 | | 90 | |

3 (a) Complete the number pattern.

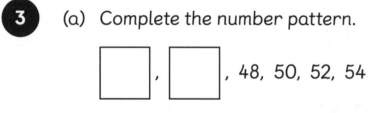 , , 48, 50, 52, 54

(b) Explain how you worked out the missing numbers.

Name: _____ Class: _____ Date: _____

Roll an 8-sided dice until you have 3 different digits.
Write down the digits.

☐ ☐ ☐

Use the digits to fill in the blanks below.

The smallest 2-digit number I can make is ☐ .

The greatest 2-digit number I can make is ☐ .

Make two more 2-digit numbers.

☐ ☐

Arrange the numbers in order.

☐ , ☐ , ☐ , ☐

greatest ⟶ smallest

Name: _____ Class: _____ Date: _____

Review 15

1 Count and fill in the blanks.

(a)

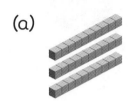

[ ] tens = [ ]

(b)

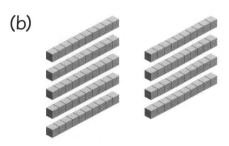

[ ] tens = [ ]

2 Fill in the blanks.

(a)

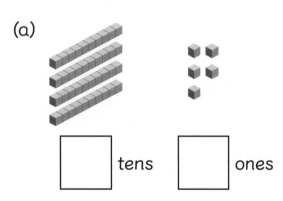

[ ] tens   [ ] ones

tens	ones

(b)

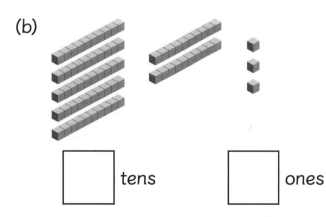

[ ] tens   [ ] ones

tens	ones

3 (a) Arrange the numbers in order from smallest to greatest.

(i)

| 72 | 67 | 60 |

☐ , ☐ , ☐

(ii)

| 32 | 34 | 31 |

☐ , ☐ , ☐

(b) Arrange the numbers in order from greatest to smallest.

(i)

| 35 | 42 | 29 |

☐ , ☐ , ☐

(ii)

| 24 | 28 | 22 |

☐ , ☐ , ☐

4 Complete the number bonds and match.

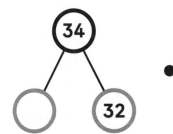

●   ● The whole is 1 less than 40.

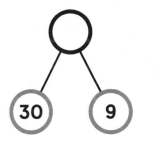

●   ● The whole is 5 more than 30.

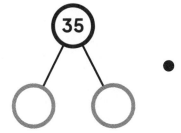

●   ● The whole is 2 more than 32.

5 Complete the number patterns.

(a) 58, ☐ , 62, 64, 66, 68

(b) 93, 91, ☐ , 87, 85, 83

(c) ☐ , 60, 70, 80, 90

6 Fill in the blanks.

(a) The value of 5 in 75 is ☐ .

(b) The value of 9 in 98 is ☐ .

7 Write in words.

(a) | 52 | |

(b) | 48 | |

Revision 3

1 Count in tens and ones.
Write the missing numbers. Write the numbers in words.

(a)

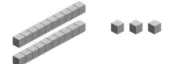

23 = [ ] tens [ ] ones

tens	ones

23 in words is [   ]

(b)

36 = [ ] tens [ ] ones

tens	ones

36 in words is [   ]

(c)

[ ] = [ ] tens [ ] ones

tens	ones

[ ] in words is [   ]

2 Complete the number patterns.

(a) 25, 27, 29, [ ], 33, [ ]

(b) 22, 21, [ ], [ ], 18, [ ]

(c) 34, 32, [ ], [ ], 26, [ ]

3 Fill in the blanks.

(a) 2 more than 15 is [ ].

(b) 5 more than 47 is [ ].

(c) [ ] is 3 less than 52.

(d) [ ] is 10 less than 78.

4 Tick (✓) if all the groups are equal.

(a) 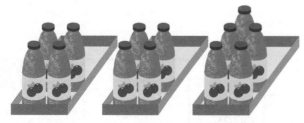 [ ]

(b) [ ]

(c) [ ]

5 Fill in the blanks.

(a)

Double 4 = ⬜ fours

= ⬜

(b) Double 7 = ⬜ sevens

= ⬜

(c) Double 9 = ⬜ nines

= ⬜

6 Write the missing numbers.

(a) Circle groups of 5 dots.

There are ⬜ groups of 5 dots.

(b) Sam has 15 tennis balls.
He puts 3 tennis balls in each tube.
How many tubes of tennis balls does Sam fill?

Sam fills ⬜ tubes of tennis balls.

Help  write the missing numbers.

(c) There are 9 basketballs.
They are shared equally between 3 children.
How many basketballs does each child get?

Each child gets ☐ basketballs.

(d)

(i)   There are ☐ cookies.

(ii) The cookies can be put into ☐ groups of 2 cookies.

(iii) The cookies can be put into ☐ groups of 3 cookies.

(iv) The cookies can be put into ☐ groups of 4 cookies.

(v)   The cookies can be put into ☐ groups of 6 cookies.

7 (a) Shade half of the square.

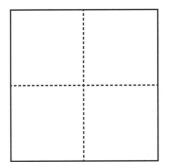

(b) Shade a quarter of the triangle.

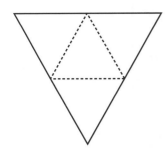

8 Write the missing numbers.

(a)

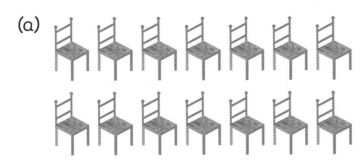

Half of the chairs = [ ] chairs

(b)

A quarter of the tables = [ ] tables

9 Write the missing numbers in the 100-square.

1	2		4	5	6	7	8	9	10
11	12	13	14	15	16	17	18	19	
21	22	23	24	25	26	27	28	29	30
31	32	33	34	35	36	37	38	39	40
41	42	43	44	45	46	47	48	49	50
51	52	53			56	57	58	59	60
61	62	63	64	65	66	67	68	69	70
71	72	73	74	75	76	77	78	79	
	82	83	84	85	86	87	88	89	90
91	92	93	94	95	96	97	98	99	

10 (a) Compare 56, 65 and 54.

The greatest number is ☐ .

The smallest number is ☐ .

(b) Arrange 98, 89 and 99 in order, starting with the greatest.

☐ , ☐ , ☐

Time

Name: _____ Class: _____ Date: _____

Worksheet 1

Telling Time to the Hour

1 Write the time shown on each clock.

(a)

☐ o'clock

(b)

[ ]

(c)

[ ]

(d)

[ ]

2 Draw the missing hands on the clock to show the time.

(a)

10 o'clock

(b)

6 o'clock

(c)

1 o'clock

3 Draw the hour hand on the clock to show the time.
Draw a picture and write what you are doing at that time.
Use **morning**, **afternoon** or **evening** to complete the sentence.

For example:

I | start school | at | 9 | o'clock in the | morning .

I | | at | | o'clock in the | .

Name: _____ Class: _____ Date: _____

Worksheet 2

Telling Time to the Half Hour

1   Write the time shown on each clock.

(a)

half past ☐

(b)

☐

(c)

☐

(d)

☐

2   Draw the missing hands on the clock to show the time.

(a)

half past 11

(b)

half past 6

(c)

half past 3

3　Draw the hour hand on the clock to show the time.
Draw a picture and write what you are doing at that time.
Use **morning, afternoon** or **night** to complete the sentence.

For example:

I | brush my teeth | at half past | 7 | in the | evening | .

I | | at half past | | in the | | .

Worksheet 3

Ordering Events

1 Complete the sentences using **before** or **after**.

(a) Sam peels a banana [   ] eating it.

(b) Emma ties her laces [   ] putting on her shoe.

(c) Oak eats breakfast at home [   ] going to school.

(d) Jacob wraps the present [   ] tying a bow.

(e) Ruby walks home [   ] school ends.

(f) Charles sets the table [   ] dinner.

2 The pictures show Ravi's activities on a Sunday.

eat breakfast

play football

go home

visit friends

go to park

walk home

dinner with family

watch television

go to bed

Fill in the blanks.

(a) Ravi first eats breakfast at [   ].

(b) At half past nine, Ravi [   ].

(c) Ravi goes home at [   ] after playing football.

(d) Ravi [   ] at 1 o'clock.

(e) At [   ], Ravi goes to the park with his friends.

(f) Ravi [   ] at 4 o'clock.

(g) Ravi has dinner at [   ] with his family.

(h) After dinner, Ravi [   ] at half past 8.

(i) Ravi goes to bed at [   ].

3 Complete the sentences using activities you do at that time.

 First, _____
_____
_____

 Next, _____
_____
_____

 After, _____
_____
_____

 Then, _____
_____
_____

Chapter 16 | Worksheet 3: Ordering Events

Worksheet 4

Estimating Duration of Time

1 Complete the sentences using **seconds**, **minutes** or **hours**.

(a) It takes Holly about 2 [   ] to brush her teeth.

(b) Sam can write his name in 5 [   ].

(c) Lulu sleeps for about 10 [   ] every night.

(d) It takes Elliott 6 [   ] to drink a glass of water.

(e) Amira can read a picture book in 20 [   ].

(f) Oak spends 2 [   ] in an art class on Saturday.

2 Complete the sentences using **hours** or **days**.

(a) The drive from Liverpool to Birmingham is about

2 ☐ long.

(b) A flight from Manchester to New York is about

8 ☐ long.

(c) Ravi goes to school for 5 ☐ every week.

(d) It takes about 7 ☐ for grass seeds to grow.

3 Complete the sentences using **seconds, minutes, hours, days** or **weeks**.

(a) Driving from Brighton to Bristol takes about 3 ☐.

(b) The summer holidays are about 6 ☐ long.

(c) It takes about 4 ☐ to fill a glass with water.

(d) Jacob spends 8 ☐ preparing his lunch.

(e) The outdoor market will be open for 2 ☐ next week.

Name: _____ Class: _____ Date: _____

Comparing Time

1 Compare using **quicker** or **slower**.

(a) The 🐢 is [   ] than the 🐇.

(b) The 🐑 is [   ] than the 🐇.

(c) The 🐇 is [   ] than the 🐑.

2 These are the times three different trains arrive at Birmingham station in the afternoon.

Compare using **earlier** or **later**.

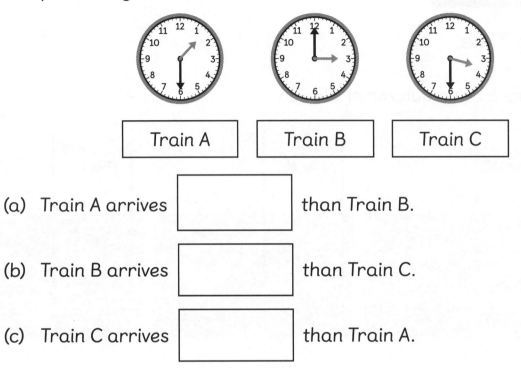

| Train A | Train B | Train C |

(a) Train A arrives [   ] than Train B.

(b) Train B arrives [   ] than Train C.

(c) Train C arrives [   ] than Train A.

(d) Train B arrives [   ] than Train A.

3 These are the times three different trains depart Birmingham station in the morning.

Write two sentences using **earlier** or **later**.

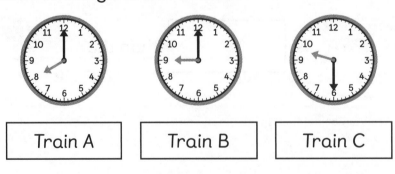

| Train A | Train B | Train C |

1. _____

2. _____

Worksheet 6

Using a Calendar

1

	June 2022					
M	T	W	T	F	S	S
		1	2	3	4	5
6	7	8	9	10	11	12
13	14	15	16	17	18	19
20	21	22	23	24	25	26
27	28	29	30			

Use the calendar to complete the sentences.

(a)   The first day of June is a ⬚ .

(b)   There are ⬚ days in June.

(c)   The last day of June is a ⬚ .

(d)   Circle the 3rd Saturday of the month.

(e)   There are ⬚ complete weekends in June.

2 Fill in the blanks.

(a) There are ☐ days in a week.

(b) Monday is the day after ☐ .

(c) ☐ and ☐ are the days of the weekend.

3 Complete the sentences.

(a) Tuesday is the day before ☐ .

(b) There are ☐ months in a year.

(c) The shortest month of the year is ☐ .

(d) The last month of the year is ☐ .

Mind Challenge

Calendar 2022

January

M	T	W	T	F	S	S
					1	2
3	4	5	6	7	8	9
10	11	12	13	14	15	16
17	18	19	20	21	22	23
24	25	26	27	28	29	30
31						

February

M	T	W	T	F	S	S
	1	2	3	4	5	6
7	8	9	10	11	12	13
14	15	16	17	18	19	20
21	22	23	24	25	26	27
28						

March

M	T	W	T	F	S	S
	1	2	3	4	5	6
7	8	9	10	11	12	13
14	15	16	17	18	19	20
21	22	23	24	25	26	27
28	29	30	31			

April

M	T	W	T	F	S	S
				1	2	3
4	5	6	7	8	9	10
11	12	13	14	15	16	17
18	19	20	21	22	23	24
25	26	27	28	29	30	

May

M	T	W	T	F	S	S
						1
2	3	4	5	6	7	8
9	10	11	12	13	14	15
16	17	18	19	20	21	22
23	24	25	26	27	28	29
30	31					

June

M	T	W	T	F	S	S
	1	2	3	4	5	
6	7	8	9	10	11	12
13	14	15	16	17	18	19
20	21	22	23	24	25	26
27	28	29	30			

July

M	T	W	T	F	S	S
				1	2	3
4	5	6	7	8	9	10
11	12	13	14	15	16	17
18	19	20	21	22	23	24
25	26	27	28	29	30	31

August

M	T	W	T	F	S	S
1	2	3	4	5	6	7
8	9	10	11	12	13	14
15	16	17	18	19	20	21
22	23	24	25	26	27	28
29	30	31				

September

M	T	W	T	F	S	S
		1	2	3	4	
5	6	7	8	9	10	11
12	13	14	15	16	17	18
19	20	21	22	23	24	25
26	27	28	29	30		

October

M	T	W	T	F	S	S
					1	2
3	4	5	6	7	8	9
10	11	12	13	14	15	16
17	18	19	20	21	22	23
24	25	26	27	28	29	30
31						

November

M	T	W	T	F	S	S
	1	2	3	4	5	6
7	8	9	10	11	12	13
14	15	16	17	18	19	20
21	22	23	24	25	26	27
28	29	30				

December

M	T	W	T	F	S	S
			1	2	3	4
5	6	7	8	9	10	11
12	13	14	15	16	17	18
19	20	21	22	23	24	25
26	27	28	29	30	31	

Can you guess the correct day, date and month in the calendar?

It is in the month just before July.

It is the day after Thursday.

A week before this date was the 10th.

Review 16

1 Match.

    ●   ●   half past 7

   ●   ●   8 o'clock

   ●   ●   4 o'clock

   ●   ●   2 o'clock

   ●   ●   half past 3

2 The pictures show what Ruby does on a Saturday.
Write the time shown on each clock.

(a)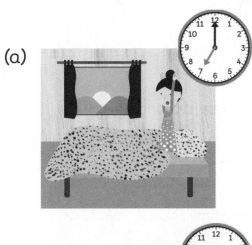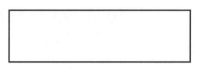

[box]

(b)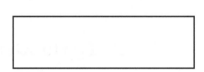

[box]

(c)

[box]

(d)

[box]

3 Complete the sentences using **seconds**, **minutes**, **hours**, **days** or **weeks**.

(a) Playtime is about 15 ⬚.

(b) It takes about 20 ⬚ to peel an orange.

(c) I am at school for about 6 ⬚ each day.

(d) The summer holiday lasts about 6 ⬚.

(e) I go to school 5 ⬚ a week.

4 (a) There are ⬚ days in October.

October 2022						
M	T	W	T	F	S	S
					1	2
3	4	5	6	7	8	9
10	11	12	13	14	15	16
17	18	19	20	21	22	23
24	25	26	27	28	29	30
31						

(b) The first day of October is a ⬚.

(c) The last day of October is a ⬚.

(d) There are ⬚ complete weeks in October.

(e) Circle the third Wednesday in October.

(f) The first day of November 2022 is a ⬚.

Money

Chapter 17

Name: _____ Class: _____ Date: _____

Worksheet 1

Recognising Coins

1 Ravi has coins from different countries.
Circle the coins from the United Kingdom.

2 Match.

 £1 •

 50 •

 10 •

 20 •

 £2 •

• 50 pence

• 2 pounds

• 10 pence

• 1 pound

• 20 pence

3 Which of these coins has a value greater than £1?

The [ ] coin has a value greater than £1.

Name: _____ Class: _____ Date: _____

Worksheet 2

Recognising Notes

1 Colour the 5 pound note blue.
Colour the 10 pound note orange.
Colour the 20 pound note purple.
Colour the 50 pound note red.

2   (a)   Match.

   •   •   5 pounds

   •   •   50 pounds

   •   •   10 pounds

   •   •   20 pounds

(b)   Match.

•   •   5 pounds

•   •   50 pounds

•   •   10 pounds

•   •   20 pounds

3 Who can buy the greatest number of footballs?

£5 each

Lulu

Charles

Sam

Mind Challenge

Which notes can Elliott use to pay for the bag?

£25

Review 17

1 Circle the coins with a value of less than 50 pence.

2 Fill in the blanks.

(a) There are ☐ 1 pound coins.   (b) There are ☐ 10 pound notes.

(c) There are ☐ 20 pence coins.   (d) There are ☐ 5 pound notes.

3 Match.

•

• 50 pence

•

• 20 pence

•

• 5 pounds

•

• 2 pounds

•

• 20 pounds

•

• 5 pence

4

I think I have more money than you.

Lulu

I think I have more money than you.

Charles

Who is correct?
Explain your answer.

_____ is correct because _____

_____

_____

Volume and Capacity

Chapter 18

Name: _____ Class: _____ Date: _____

Worksheet 1

Comparing Volume

1 Circle the containers that are full.
Cross out the containers that are empty.

2 Compare using **more than**, **less than** or **equal to**.

A   B   C

The amount of milk in bottle A is [   ] the amount of milk in bottle B.

The amount of milk in bottle B is [   ] the amount of milk in bottle C.

3 Match the children with the correct jug.

My jug is full.

My jug has less juice than Sam's jug.

My jug has more juice than Holly's jug.

Worksheet 2

Finding Capacity

1 Elliott uses  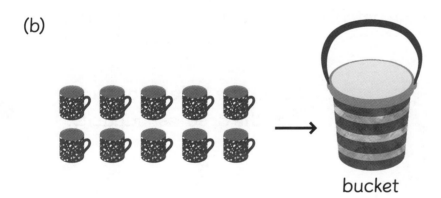 to fill the containers completely.

Each ☕ is 1 unit.

(a)

The capacity of the bottle is about ☐ units.

bottle

(b)

The capacity of the bucket is about ☐ units.

bucket

2 Amira pours all the water from each container into 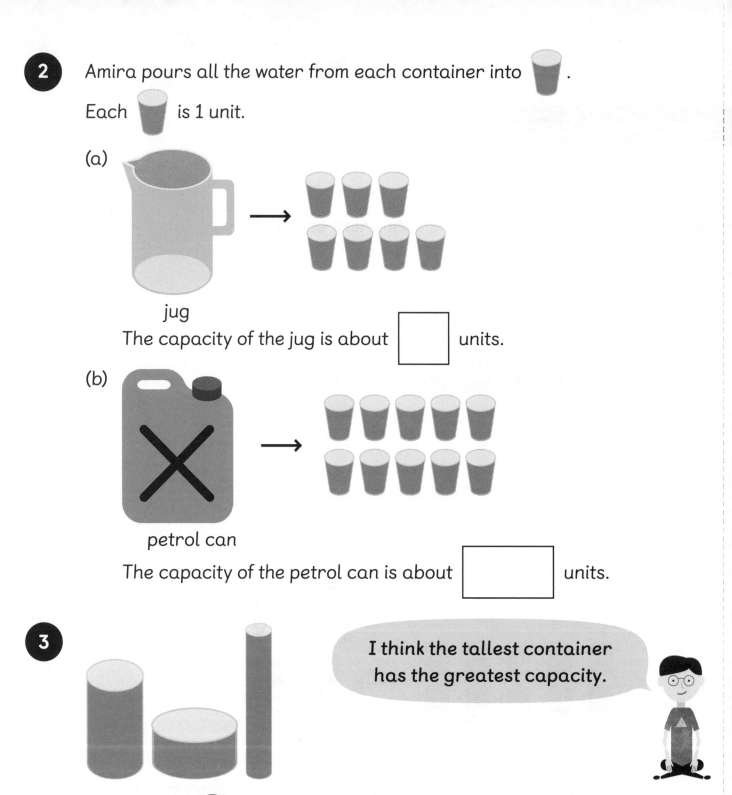.

Each 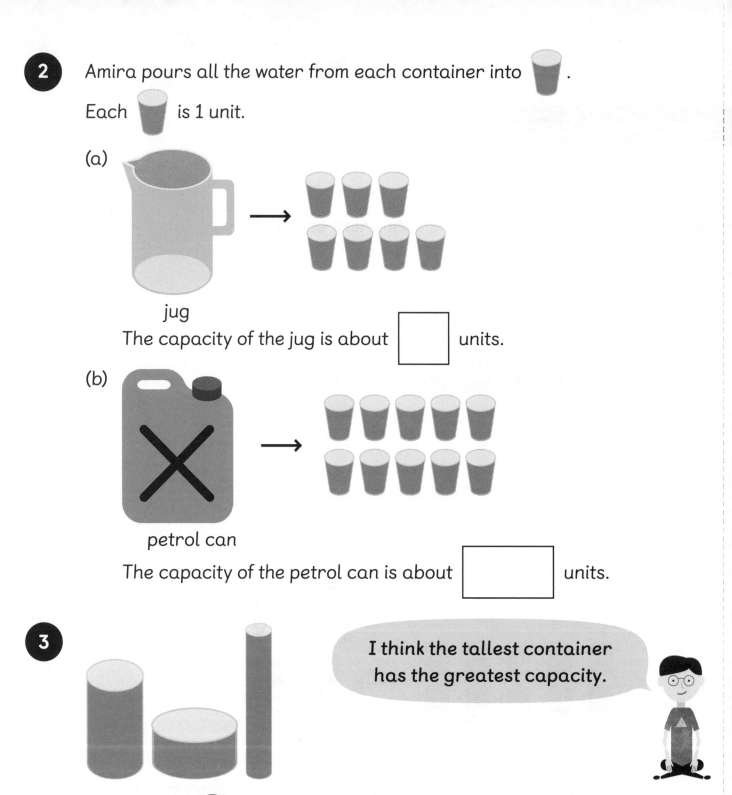 is 1 unit.

(a)

jug

The capacity of the jug is about ☐ units.

(b)

petrol can

The capacity of the petrol can is about ☐ units.

3

> I think the tallest container has the greatest capacity.

Do you think 😊 is correct?

Explain your answer using words and pictures.

Name: _____ Class: _____ Date: _____

Worksheet 3

Describing Volume Using Half and a Quarter

1 Ruby uses the smaller containers to completely fill the larger containers. Complete the sentences using **half** or **a quarter**.

(a)

mugs   bottle

The capacity of 1 mug is [   ] of the capacity of the bottle.

(b)

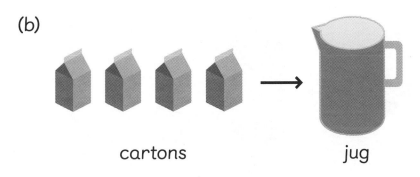

cartons   jug

The capacity of 1 carton is [   ] of the capacity of the jug.

The capacity of 2 cartons is [   ] of the capacity of the jug.

2 Emma uses 4 to completely fill  .

Circle the number of needed to:

(a) fill half of the jug

(b) fill a quarter of the jug

3 It takes 4 mugs to completely fill the carton.

mugs   carton

1 mug makes the carton a quarter full.
2 mugs make the carton half full.
Do you agree or disagree?
Explain your answer using words and pictures.

Mind Challenge

The pictures show the capacities of each container.

How many are needed to fill the bucket?

Name: _____ Class: _____ Date: _____

1 Compare using **more than, less than, full** or **empty**.

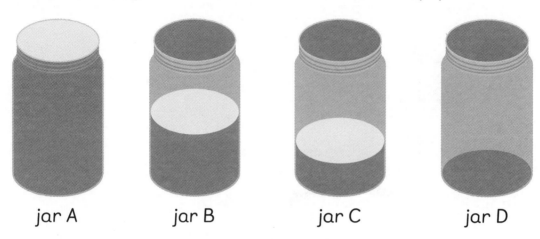

jar A   jar B   jar C   jar D

(a) Jar A is [   ] of water.

(b) The amount of water in jar B is [   ] the amount of water in jar C.

(c) The amount of water in jar C is [   ] the amount of water in jar A.

(d) Jar D is [   ].

2 The pictures show the the number of 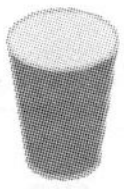 Ravi needs to fill each bottle completely.
Fill in the blanks using **half** or **a quarter**.

(a)

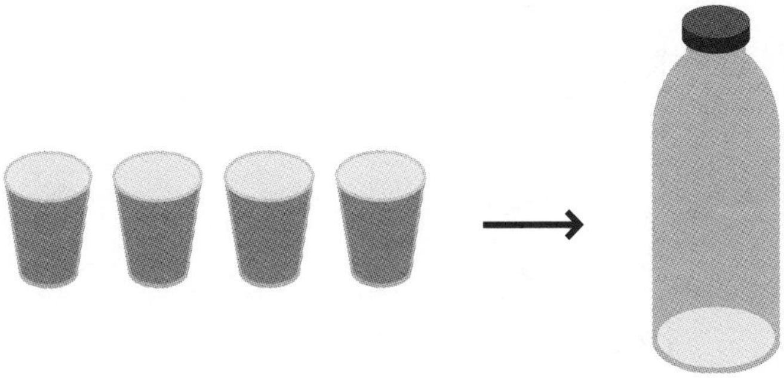

The capacity of 1 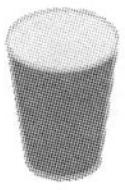 is ________ of the capacity of the bottle.

(b)

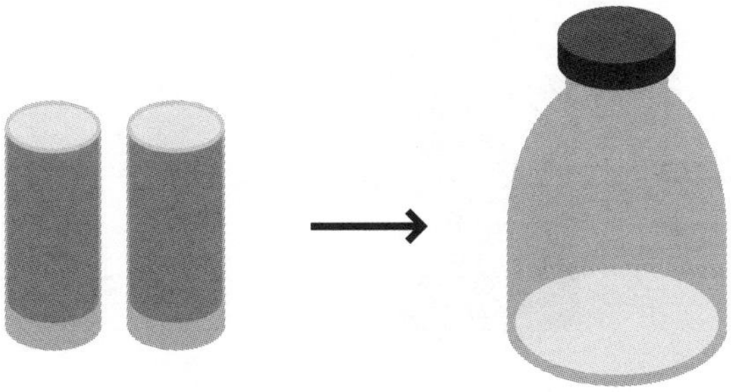

The capacity of 1  is ________ of the capacity of the bottle.

(c)

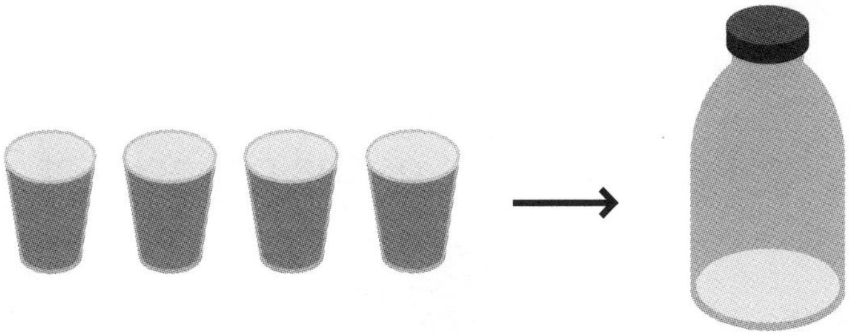

The capacity of 2 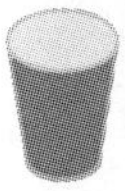 is ________ of the capacity of the bottle.

3 Draw the water levels in the beakers to show the following:
Beaker A has more water than beaker B.
Beaker C has less water than beaker A.

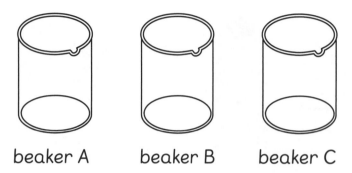

beaker A   beaker B   beaker C

4 Circle the correct number of .

(a) The capacity of the kettle is the same as the capacity of 6 ☕.

(b) The capacity of the bowl is the same as the capacity of 2 ☕.

(c) The capacity of the bottle is the same as the capacity of 5 ☕.

Mass

Name: _____ Class: _____ Date: _____

Worksheet 1

Comparing Mass

1 Match.

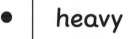 heavy

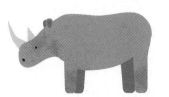

light

2  is comparing the mass of some objects.

Help him fill in the blanks using **heavier than**, **lighter than** or **as heavy as**.

(a)

The bag of flour is [ ] the chocolate bar.

(b)

The cookie is [ ] the book.

(c)

The football is [ ] the teddy bear.

3 Look at the balance scales.
Correct the sentences using **heavier than, lighter than** or **as heavy as**.

(a)

The sack of potatoes is as heavy as the lollipop.

Correct sentence: _____

_____

(b)

The box of crackers is heavier than the block of cheese.

Correct sentence: _____

_____

(c)

The pencil case is lighter than the roll of tape.

Correct sentence: _____

_____

(d)

3 toy cars weigh the same as 2 toy aeroplanes.

(i) A toy car is [   ] a toy aeroplane.

(ii) 6 toy cars are [   ] 2 toy aeroplanes.

Name: _____ Class: _____ Date: _____

Worksheet 2

Finding Mass

1 Help  count the blocks and write the mass of the object.

1 🔲 shows 1 unit.

The mass of the eraser is about ☐ units.

2 Write the mass.

1 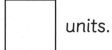 shows 1 unit.

(a)

The mass of the tomatoes is about ☐ units.

(b)

The mass of 1 banana is about [ ] units.

3   Look at the balance scales.
Are the statements true or false?
Circle the correct answer.

1 ● shows 1 unit.

(a)   The lettuce is heavier than 3 carrots.   (true / false)

(b)   The melon is lighter than the lettuce.   (true / false)

(c)   The lettuce is as heavy as the melon.   (true / false)

(d)   3 carrots are heavier than the melon.   (true / false)

(e)   The lettuce is the lightest.   (true / false)

(f)   The melon is the heaviest.   (true / false)

Chapter 19 | Worksheet 2: Finding Mass

Name: _____ Class: _____ Date: _____

Worksheet 3

Finding and Comparing Mass

Fill in the blanks.

The ruler is about 3 units.

The sharpener is about 2 units.

The ruler is ☐ (lighter / heavier) than

the sharpener.

3 units is more than 2 units.
2 units is less than 3 units.

The sharpener is ☐ (lighter / heavier) than

the ruler.

2

The apple is about 6 units.

The mango is about 9 units.

☐ units is more than ☐ units.

☐ units less than ☐ units.

The mango is ☐ (lighter / heavier) than the apple.

The apple is ☐ (lighter / heavier) than

the mango.

3

book

glue stick

The ☐ is heavier than the ☐ .

Mind Challenge

Find the mass of the cake.

The mass of the bunch of grapes is ☐ .

The mass of the box of biscuits is ☐ .

The mass of the cake is ☐ .

Review 19

1 Group each of the following into heavy and light objects.

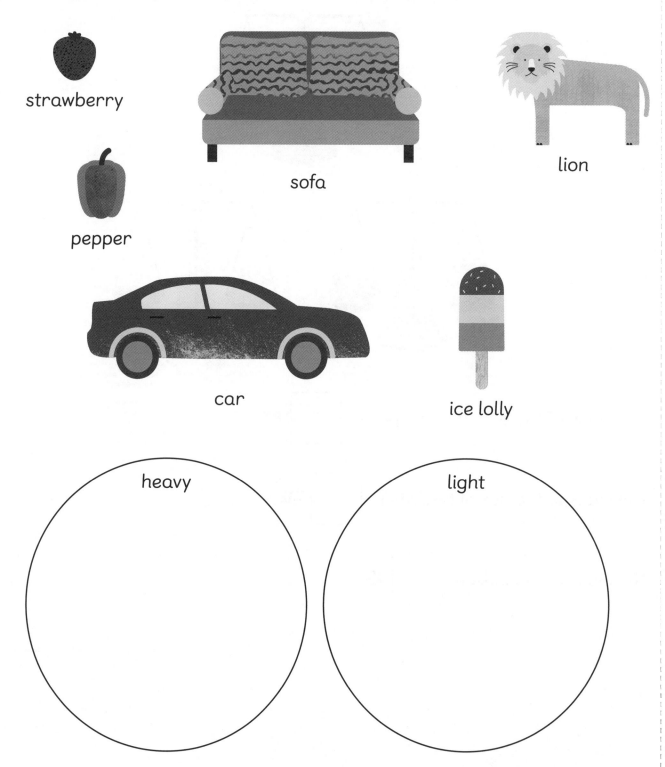

strawberry

pepper

sofa

lion

car

ice lolly

heavy

light

2 Compare the mass of the objects using **heavier than, lighter than** or **as heavy as**.

(a)

The golf ball is [   ] 2 pens.

(b)

The toy car is [   ] the football.

(c)

The doll is [   ] the balloon.

3 Count.

1 shows 1 unit.

(a)

The mass of the coconut

is about ☐ units.

(b)

The mass of the bag of apples

is about ☐ units.

4

(a) The mass of 1 orange is ☐ units.

(b) The mass of 1 mango is ☐ units.

(c) The mass of 1 coconut is ☐ units.

Space

Chapter 20

Name: _____ Class: _____ Date: _____

Worksheet 1

Describing Positions

1 Describe using **top, middle** and **bottom**.

(a) The fruits are on the [＿＿＿＿＿] shelf.

(b) The meat is on the [＿＿＿＿＿] shelf.

(c) The cheese is on the [＿＿＿＿＿] shelf.

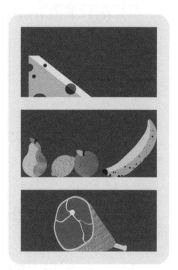

2 Describe using **on top of, in front of** and **above**.

(a) The sun is [＿＿＿＿＿] the clouds.

(b) Charles is sitting [＿＿＿＿＿] the donkey.

(c) The bucket is [＿＿＿＿＿] the donkey.

3 Use the picture to answer the questions below.

Sam   Charles   Ruby

(a) Fill in the blanks using **near** and **far from**.

Sam is [ ] Ruby.

Charles is [ ] the tree.

(b) Fill in the blanks using **around** and **close to**.

The flowers are [ ] the tree.

Charles is [ ] the swings.

(c) Fill in the blanks using **left**, **right** and **between**.

The swings are [ ] Sam and Charles.

The slide is to the [ ] of the tree.

The tree is to the [ ] of the slide.

Name: _____ Class: _____ Date: _____

Worksheet 2

Describing Movements

1 Fill in the blanks using **forwards**, **backwards**, **up** and **down**.

(a)

Sam is running [_____] the hill.

(b)

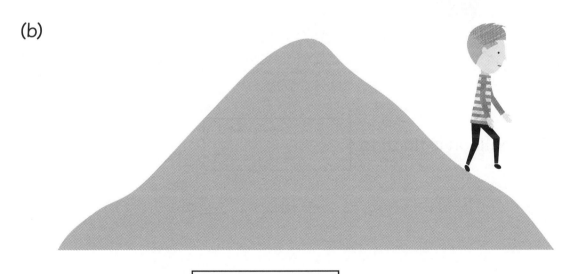

Sam is walking [_____] the hill.

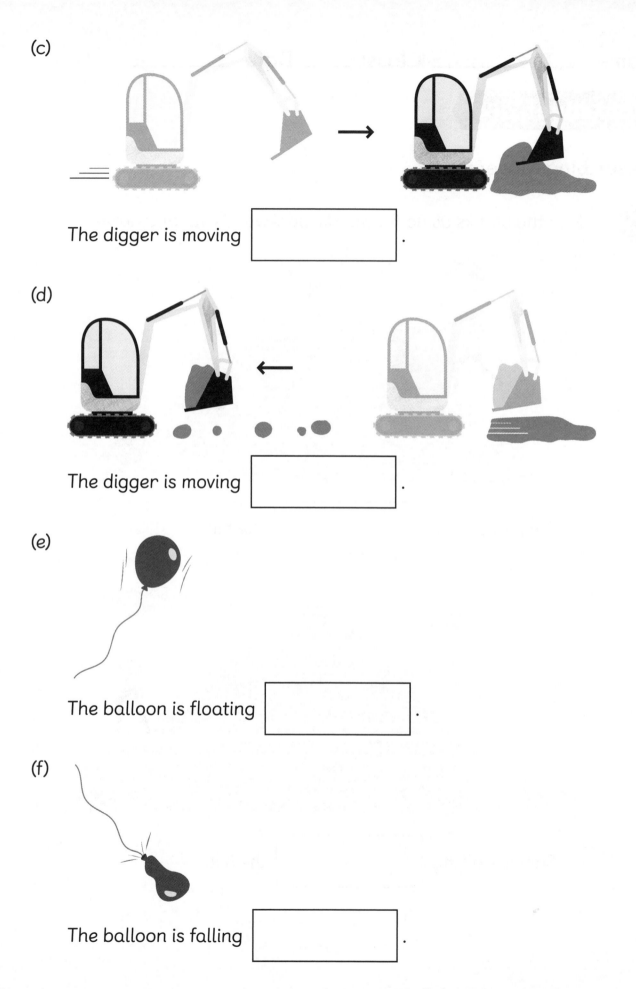

(c)

The digger is moving [   ] .

(d)

The digger is moving [   ] .

(e)

The balloon is floating [   ] .

(f)

The balloon is falling [   ] .

2 Describe using **outside** and **inside**.

(a)

The egg is [ ] the carton.

(b)

The egg is [ ] the carton.

(c)

The dog is [ ] the kennel.

(d)

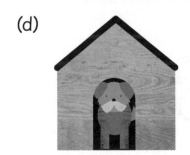

The dog is [ ] the kennel.

3 Look at the picture, then write the correct sentence.

(a)

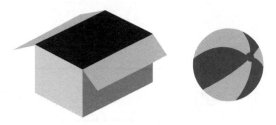

The ball is inside the box.

Correct sentence: _____

_____

(b)

The pancake is down in the air.

Correct sentence: _____

_____

(c)

The car is moving backwards.

Correct sentence: _____

_____

Name: _____ Class: _____ Date: _____

Making Turns

 Match.

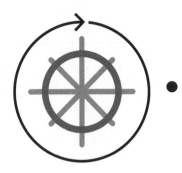

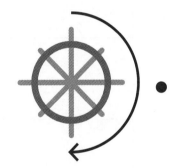

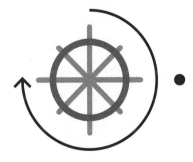

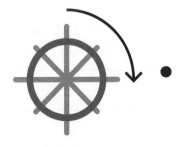

	quarter turn
	whole turn
	three-quarter turn
	half turn

2 Describe using **whole, half, quarter** and **three-quarter**.

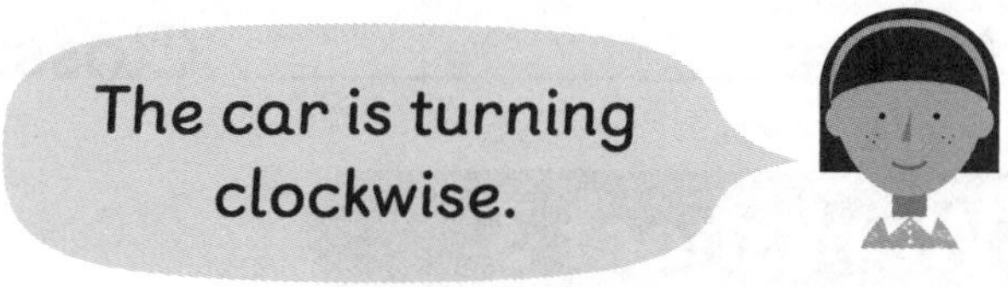

The car is turning clockwise.

[_____] turn

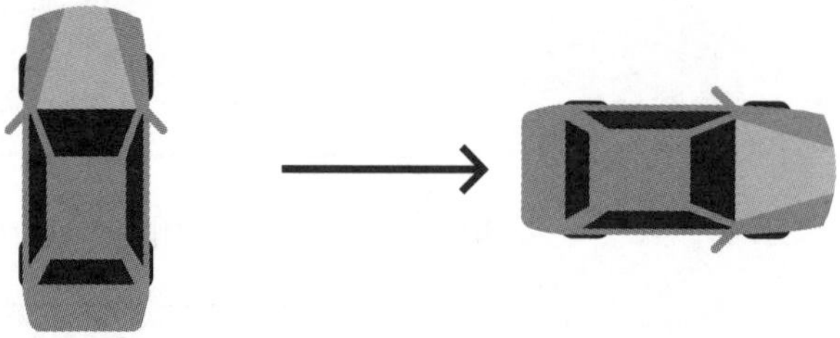

[_____] turn

[_____] turn

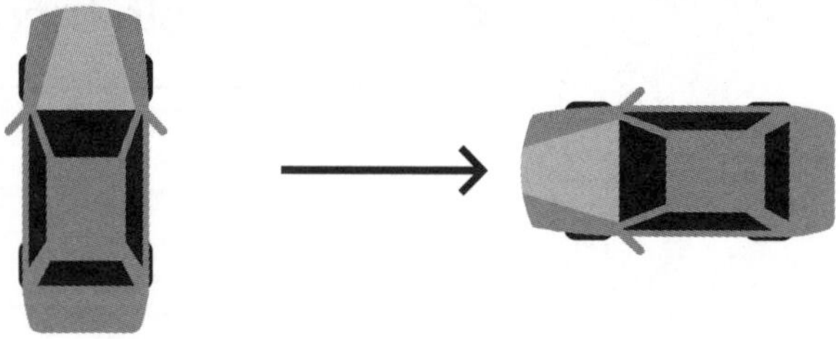

[_____] turn

3

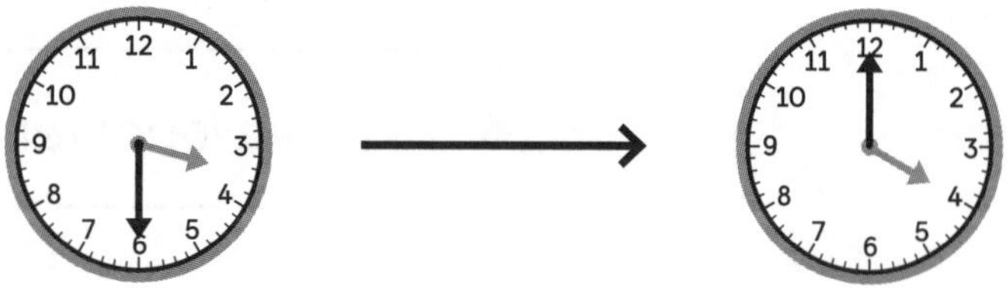

Explain how you know the minute hand has made half a turn.

_____

_____

_____

_____

Mind Challenge ▶

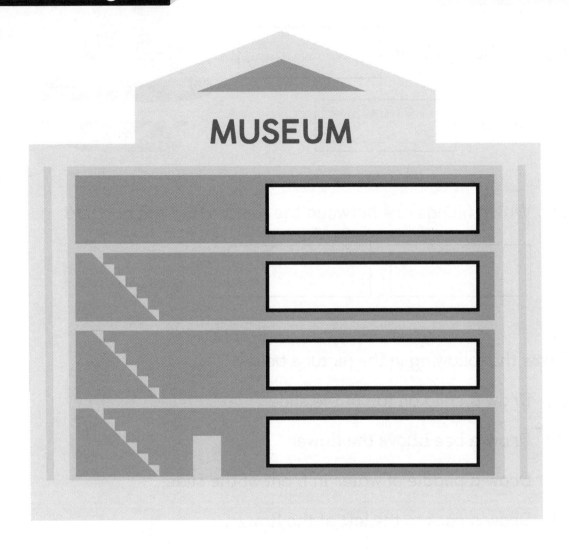

Using the information below, write the correct names in the blanks.

Amira is on the floor above Charles.
Elliott is on the bottom floor.
Lulu is on the floor above Elliott.
Lulu is on the floor below Charles.

Review 20

1 (a) The bun is at the [_____]

and the [_____] .

bun
burger
cheese
lettuce
tomato
bun

(b) Which fillings are between the tomato and the burger?

[_____] , [_____]

2 Draw the following in the picture below.

(a) Draw a child on top of the slide.

(b) Draw a bee above the flower.

(c) Draw a puddle of water in front of the slide.

(d) Draw a rock to the left of the flower.

(e) Draw a tree to the right of the slide.

3 Fill in the blanks using **up**, **down**, **forwards**, **backwards**, **inside** and **outside**.

(a)

The monkey is [ ] in the tree.

(b)

The monkey is [ ] on the ground.

(c)

The owl is [ ] the barn.

(d)

The owl is [ ] the barn.

(e)

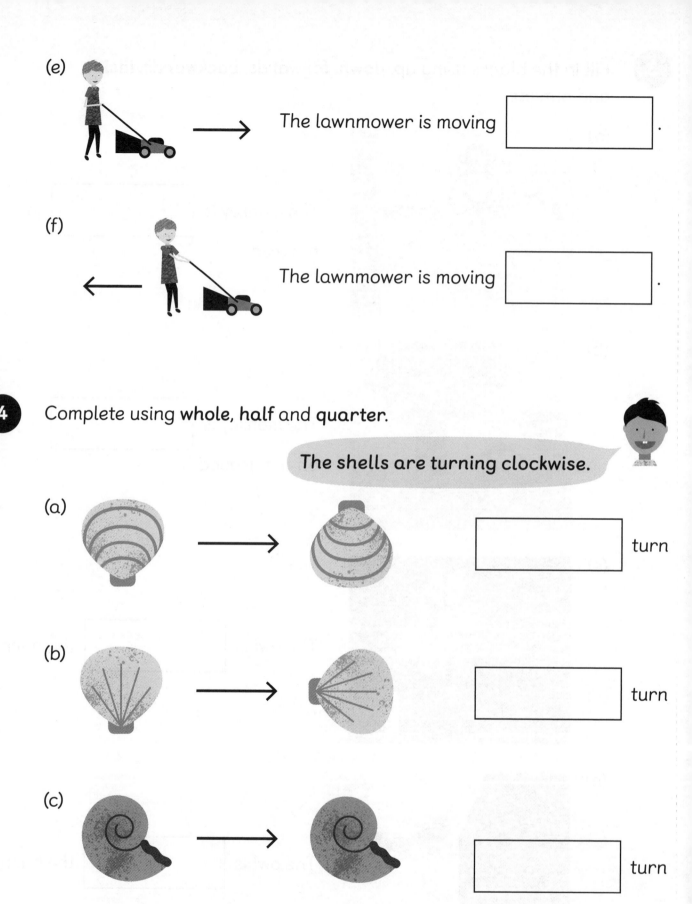

The lawnmower is moving [ ].

(f)

The lawnmower is moving [ ].

4 Complete using **whole**, **half** and **quarter**.

The shells are turning clockwise.

(a)

[ ] turn

(b)

[ ] turn

(c)

[ ] turn

Name: _____ Class: _____ Date: _____

Revision 4

1 Help write the time shown on each clock.

(a)

(b)

(c)

(d)

2 Complete.

(a) The day after Monday is _____ .

(b) The first month of the year is _____ .

3 Fill in the blanks on the calendar.

Calendar 2022

May

M	T	W	T	F	S	S
						1
2	3	4	5	6	7	8
9	10	11	12	13	14	15
16	17	18	19	20	21	22
23	24	25	26	27	28	29
30	31					

June

M	T	W	T	F	S	S
		1	2	3	4	5
6	7	8	9	10	11	12
13	14	15	16	17	18	19
20	21	22	23	24	25	26
27	28	29	30			

(blank)

M	T	W	T	F	S	S
				1	2	3
4	5	6	7	8	9	10
11	12	13	14	15	16	17
18	19	20	21	22	23	24
25	26	27	28	29	30	31

August

M	T	W	T	F	S	S
1	2	3	4	5	6	7
8	9	10	11	12	13	14
15	16	17	18	19	20	21
22	23	24	25	26	27	28
29	30	31				

(blank)

M	T	W	T	F	S	S
			1	2	3	4
5	6	7	8	9	10	11
12	13	14	15	16	17	18
19	20	21	22	23	24	25
26	27	28	29	30		

October

M	T	W	T	F	S	S
					1	2
3	4	5	6	7	8	9
10	11	12	13	14	15	16
17	18	19	20	21	22	23
24	25	26	27	28	29	30
31						

November

M	T	W	T	F	S	S
	1	2	3	4	5	6
7	8	9	10	11	12	13
14	15	16	17	18	19	20
21	22	23	24	25	26	27
28	29	30				

(blank)

M	T	W	T	F	S	S
			1	2	3	4
5	6	7	8	9	10	11
12	13	14	15	16	17	18
19	20	21	22	23	24	25
26	27	28	29	30	31	

4 What coins are these?

(a)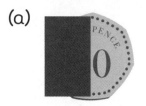

(b)

(c)

(d)

5 Circle the 20 pound note.

6 Arrange the coins from the greatest to the smallest value.

, , ,

greatest  smallest

7 Circle the container that is half full.

8 Circle the container that is a quarter full.

9 Sam pours all the water from each container into .

Each  is 1 unit.

(a)

water
bottle

The capacity of the water bottle is about ☐ units.

(b)

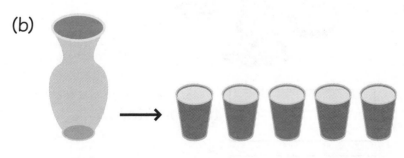

vase

The capacity of the vase is about ☐ units.

10 Circle the heavy items.

feather

bed

barrel filled
with water

cap

pencil

car

11 Fill in the blanks using **heavier than, lighter than** or **as heavy as**.

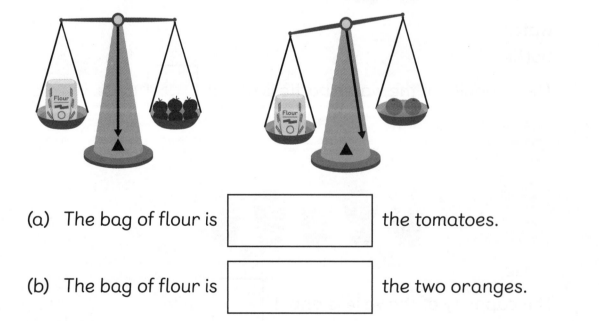

(a) The bag of flour is [   ] the tomatoes.

(b) The bag of flour is [   ] the two oranges.

12 Count.
1  shows 1 unit.

The mass of the books is about ⬚ units.

13 Fill in the blanks using **inside**, **outside** and **on top of**.

(a) The bird is ⬚ the garage.

(b) Ravi is ⬚ the garage.

(c) The car is ⬚ the garage.

14 Describe Ravi's turns using **whole, half, quarter** and **three-quarter.**

(a)

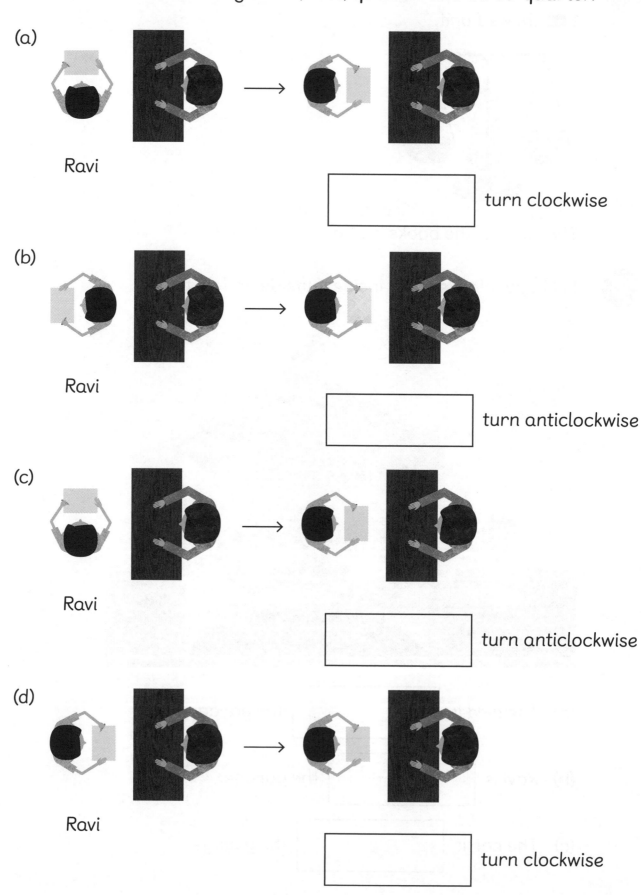

Ravi

turn clockwise

(b)

Ravi

turn anticlockwise

(c)

Ravi

turn anticlockwise

(d)

Ravi

turn clockwise

Name: _____ Class: _____ Date: _____

End-of-Year Revision

Section A
Choose the correct answer.
Write its letter in the box.

1 What number is shown?

(a) 83

(b) 53

(c) 38

(d) 35

2 Count.
Which place-value chart shows the correct number for the blocks?

(a)

tens	ones
4	8

(b)

tens	ones
4	7

(c)

tens	ones
4	5

(d)

tens	ones
7	8

3 What is the missing number?

? is 1 more than 27.

(a) 25

(b) 26

(c) 28

(d) 29

4 How many groups of 4 cars are there?

(a) 3

(b) 4

(c) 8

(d) 12

5 What is the missing number?

3 groups of 5 = ?

(a) 18

(b) 15

(c) 9

(d) 8

End-of-Year Revision

6 What is the missing number?

37, 39, [?] , 43, 45

(a) 40

(b) 41

(c) 42

(d) 44

[ ]

7 What time does the clock show?

(a) half past 6

(b) 7 o'clock

(c) 8 o'clock

(d) half past 7

[ ]

8 Which is the 20 pence coin?

(a)    (b)    (c)    (d)

[ ]

9 What is the mass of the ball?
1  shows 1 unit.

The mass of the ball is about ⌐?⌐ units.

(a) 1

(b) 3

(c) 4

(d) 6

10 Which is the correct type of turn?

(a) whole

(b) half

(c) quarter

(d) three-quarter

Section B

Write your answers in the answer boxes provided.

11 Write the number shown in words.

12 Compare the numbers.

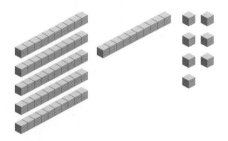 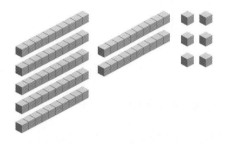

tens	ones

tens	ones

□ = □ tens □ ones   □ = □ tens □ ones

□ is more than □ .

13 Complete the number bonds.

(a)
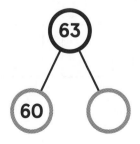

(b)
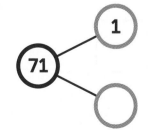

(c)
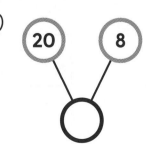

14 Fill in the blanks.

(a) 10 + ⬜ = 14

(b) 10 – ⬜ = 4

15 Fill in the blanks.

(a) 6 + 1 = ⬜

(b) ⬜ + 2 = 8

(c) 6 + ⬜ = 9

(d) 6 + ⬜ = 10

16 Compare the numbers.

(a) 74 is more than ⬜ .

(b) 74 is less than ⬜ .

(c) The smallest number is ⬜ .

(d) The greatest number is ⬜ .

17 Arrange the numbers in order.

(a) Start with the greatest.

72, 85, 58

⬜ , ⬜ , ⬜

(b) Start with the smallest.

63, 12, 26

⬜ , ⬜ , ⬜

18 Fill in the blanks.

$$\longleftarrow \mid\!\!\!\longrightarrow$$

65 66 67 68 69 70 71 72 73 74 75 76 77 78 79 80 81 82 83 84 85

(a) ☐ is 2 more than 69.   (b) ☐ is 2 less than 67.

(c) ☐ is 5 more than 78.   (d) ☐ is 5 less than 76.

19 Complete the number patterns.

(a) 51, 53, 55, ☐ , 59, ☐ , 63

(b) 74, ☐ , 70, ☐ , 66, 64, 62, ☐

20 Circle the 2D shape that does not belong.

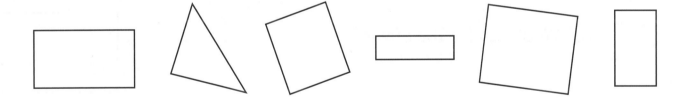

21 Circle the object that is a cuboid.

22 Circle the 3rd cup and cross out the 7th cup.

first cup

23 The children are queueing up to board the train.

Emma   Jacob   Lulu   Holly   Sam   Amira

(a) Who is 2nd in the queue?

(b) Who is 3 places ahead of Lulu?

(c) Who is 2nd from the end of the queue?

End-of-Year Revision

24 (a)

(b)

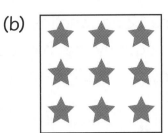 

double 6 = ☐ sixes

= ☐

double 9 = ☐ nines

= ☐

25 Circle the hats to make equal groups of 4.

There are ☐ equal groups of 4 hats.

26 There are 4 bags of bread rolls.
Each bag has 5 bread rolls.

4 groups of ☐ = ☐

☐ fives = ☐

There are ☐ bread rolls altogether.

27 There are 12 paperclips.
Put them equally into 3 groups.
How many paperclips are there in each group?

There are ☐ paperclips in each group.

28 Holly puts 6 marbles in each bag.
How many bags does Holly need?

Holly needs ☐ bags.

29 Shade a quarter of the large rectangle.

End-of-Year Revision

30 Shade half of the triangles.

△ △ △ △ △
△ △ △ △ △

31 Shade a quarter of the circles.

○ ○ ○ ○
○ ○ ○ ○
○ ○ ○ ○

32 Write the time shown on each clock.

(a)

(b)

(c)

33 Complete the sentences.

(a) The 8th month of the year is [   ].

(b) The month after March is [   ].

(c) The month before November is [   ].

34 Use the calendar to fill in the blanks.

December						
M	T	W	T	F	S	S
			1	2	3	4
5	6	7	8	9	10	11
12	13	14	15	16	17	18
19	20	21	22	23	24	25
26	27	28	29	30	31	

(a) There are ☐ Wednesdays in December.

(b) The first day of December is a ☐ .

(c) The last day of December is a ☐ .

35 Look at the coins.
Fill in the blanks.

(a) There are ☐ 10 pence coins.

(b) There are ☐ 20 pence coins.

36 What note is this?

37 Measure.

Each is 1 unit.

The capacity of is about [ ] units.

38 Oak uses the smaller containers to completely fill the larger containers. Fill in the blanks using **half** or **a quarter**.

(a)

cups   bowl

The capacity of one cup is [ ] of the capacity of the bowl.

(b)

bottles   jug

After one bottle is poured into the jug, the jug is [ ] full.

39 Compare using **heavier** or **lighter**.

(a)

The tablet is [   ]

than the phone.

(b)

The spoon is [   ]

than the plate.

40 Fill in the blanks with **to the left of, on top of** and **between**.

(a) The cat is [   ] the chair.

(b) The ball is [   ] the toy robot.

(c) The bed is [   ] the chair and the ball.

Section C
Solve the word problems.
Show your work clearly.

 41 Ruby has 9 apples.
Emma has 6 apples.
How many apples do they have altogether?

☐ ○ ☐ = ☐

Ruby and Emma have ☐ apples altogether.

42 Holly has 14 teddy bears.
She gives 6 teddy bears to Sam.
How many teddy bears does Holly have left?

☐ ○ ☐ = ☐

Holly has ☐ teddy bears left.

43 There are 5 sausages in each packet.
How many sausages are there in 4 packets?

There are ☐ sausages altogether.

44 Jacob put 12 books equally onto 3 shelves.

There are ☐ books on each shelf.

45 There are 28 strawberries.
Charles ate a quarter of the strawberries.
How many strawberries did he eat?

Charles ate ☐ strawberries.